Mind-Body Conditioning for Competitive Figure Skaters

Linda Ross, PhD

ISBN: 978-1-60679-011-3
Library of Congress Control Number: 2008934826
Cover design: Studio J Art & Design
Book layout: Studio J Art & Design
Front cover photo: ©Jeff Wheeler/Minneapolis Star Tribune/ZUMA Press

Healthy Learning
P.O. Box 1828
Monterey, CA 93942
www.healthylearning.com

Dedication

To my coach, Danette.

Acknowledgments

Several different groups of people contributed to making this program a published work, and for their efforts and input, I am most thankful. I would like to take a brief moment to acknowledge them.

First, I'd like to acknowledge my thesis committee at the University of Texas of the Permian Basin: Camille Cassidy, Lois Hale, and James Eldridge. The original program on which this book is based was part of my master's thesis in kinesiology. Dr. Eldridge, in fact, was the one who suggested publishing this work—thanks Dr. E!

I'd also like to acknowledge Cynthia Ferrara of U.S. Figure Skating's Congress on Sports Medicine and Sports Science of Figure Skating. As a member of the USFS Sports Medicine and Science National Network and presenter at the Congress on Sports Medicine and Sports Science of Figure Skating, I've had the opportunity to interact and share ideas with other sports science professionals who specialize in figure skating, as well as meet several of our nation's elite and most promising competitive figure skaters. Thanks for the opportunity to work with you.

As an adult skater, I've been enjoying the process of becoming a better skater myself and "practicing what I preach" by doing the very things I recommend in this book. However, even the most self-motivated require additional support. I was always the first to say, "I'm not here to make friends—I'm here to skate." Yet, since I've started skating as an adult, I've found a whole new social circle and network of "skating friends" at both of the rinks where I skate most frequently. Thanks to my skating friends at Sprinker and KVIC. Even though I focus pretty intensely during practice, I appreciate your friendship and our "après-skate" coffees and lunches.

Kathy Wainhouse, the Lakewood Winter Club, and the professional staff at Sprinker Recreation Center are also deserving of my thanks. Kathy gave me the opportunity to work with the talented and hard-working members of the Lakewood Winter Club and teach them many of the skills and strategies I discuss in this book. In addition, she and her staff have provided me with support both in my own skating and in the development of programs for competitive skaters. Thank you!

And lastly, my inner circle—my coaches and my husband. Glenn Patterson has inspired me to train as hard as I can and always strive to perfect every aspect of my skating. From the simplest push-off to the fine-tuning of an edge or turn, Glenn has been integral in helping me get better. Danette Green is my primary coach, my friend, and my inspiration—words cannot express the depth of my gratitude to her. She cheers me on when my confidence starts to wane, she pushes me to do it right the first time she asks, and she has instilled in me a distinct love for the sport of figure skating—as a skater, not just as a sport scientist. I couldn't imagine ever training with another coach and am so thankful to her for giving me the gift of figure skating. I am blessed to have the opportunity to train with her. And finally, my husband, Jason, who really has no interest in the sport at all, but encourages me to spread my wings and simply enjoy my training, without judgment or expectation.

Thanks to all of you, and I hope you see in this work the contributions that you've made.

Contents

Introduction

For as long as I can remember, I have been fascinated by people with extraordinary ability. It doesn't matter what their ability is in—sport, literature, mathematics, chess—all experts fascinate me. But athletes in particular, especially elite-level athletes, have always transfixed me. What I have recognized is that these athletes seem to have a common set of verbal and nonverbal behaviors. It's not just their sport performances, but how they look and speak about those experiences before, during, and afterward that is so inspiring. It's that part of being an elite athlete, not just the physical prowess, that makes those kinds of people stand out to me. And it was this inspiration that led me to study the factors that develop that type of passion, an applied branch of psychology that focuses on developing expert performance, a field known as *mind-body conditioning*.

This book is about mind-body conditioning as it applies to the artistic sport of figure skating. But as you read, you'll soon discover that mind-body conditioning skills can be applied successfully to any area of your life. I personally believe that applying mind-body conditioning techniques to all aspects of our lives makes our lives richer. We find that our experiences now seem more vivid, we seem to enjoy what we do, and, subsequently, we spend more of our time doing the things we enjoy. This idea is the concept of living with passion, which I believe is at the heart of every successful athlete. It is what I refer to as the *life-athlete* approach, where we approach challenges in our lives the same way we would approach an athletic event—with commitment, dedication, drive and desire.

Each chapter of this book begins with a description of the chapter topic, and ends with application exercises you can learn and apply to your skating and other areas of your life. Instead of trying to learn everything at once, choose the activities that make the most sense to you, and practice them until they are second nature, just like you would a skating skill. At any time, you can always go back, review a section, and revisit the exercises that you may have skipped over the first time through.

This book is for you to use and enjoy...so, continue reading, and start your journey into the highly rewarding world of bringing out the best in yourself.

About the Companion DVD

This book includes a DVD. On the DVD, you will find a yoga workout that integrates some of the skills taught in this book. The DVD also includes several other yoga-based stretching segments that you can use before or after you skate. Review the DVD at any time, or specifically when you read Chapter 8 on relaxation techniques.

Introduction to Mind-Body Conditioning

As mentioned in the Introduction, mind-body conditioning can be applied to any aspect of your life. The focus of this book is on applying these principles and techniques to the sport of figure skating. When mind-body conditioning is applied in a sport setting, it is often referred to as *applied sport psychology*, which is only one of several areas of study within the field of sport psychology. To help you get the most out of this book, a little background about sport psychology and mind-body conditioning may be helpful. This chapter addresses questions you may have about sport psychology in general and mind-body conditioning as it relates to figure skating in particular.

What Is Sport Psychology?

Sport psychology is a science in which the principles of psychology are applied in a sport setting. Sport psychologists who specialize in mind-body conditioning help people who participate in sports reach their potential as athletes. Some of the other topics that sport psychologists study include motivation, personality, leadership, and group dynamics. Sport psychologists might also teach classes, conduct research, and work directly with athletes and coaches to help improve performance and enhance the quality of the sport experience.

In short, sport psychology is the study of the effect of psychological and emotional factors on sport performance, and the effect sport involvement has on psychological and emotional factors. When described this way, you can begin to understand the interactive relationship between participating in a sport and the psychological and emotional factors involved. On the one hand, athletic performance is influenced by how you think and feel (i.e., psychological and emotional factors). Sport psychologists suggest that these factors are addressed by specific skills that can be learned and fine-tuned. On the other hand, you may also know that simply being involved in a sport like figure skating can contribute to your psychological and emotional well-being.

What Is Mind-Body Conditioning?

Mind-body conditioning focuses on identifying and applying techniques that enhance the performance and personal growth of athletes as they are practicing their *physical* skills. This approach teaches coaches and athletes how to integrate important psychological skills during practice and competition, including ways to better manage competitive stress, control concentration, improve confidence, and, in team sports, increase communication skills and team harmony. The goal of this kind of training, including the ideas discussed in this book, is to help you learn to consistently create the ideal state of being that allows you to perform at your very best.

A Little Background

The former Soviet Union countries were among the first to accept sport psychology as a legitimate sport science. In the 1950s, Russian scientists tested ancient yogic techniques with cosmonauts to help them control several bodily processes while in space. These techniques, which are now known as *self-regulation training* or *psychic self-regulation*, were used to gain voluntary control not only over bodily functions such as heart rate, temperature, and muscle tension, but also over emotional reactions to stressful situations such as being in zero gravity.

In 1978, the United States Olympic Committee (USOC) recruited advisers in four branches of sport sciences: biomechanics, exercise physiology, nutrition, and sport psychology. This development was the first time that the USOC showed an interest in using sport psychologists to help elite athletes enhance their performance. By 1983, the USOC had established an official committee and now has a registry of qualified sport psychologists.

What Do Sport Psychologists Do?

Most sport psychologists consider themselves to be educators and practitioners. They use the medium of education to teach key psychological skills to athletes and coaches. In general, their job is to help athletes develop psychological skills to improve performance during practice and competition. They also help athletes learn to enjoy their individual sport more fully and to use their sport as a vehicle for improving their quality of life.

How Are Sport Psychologists Different From Clinical or Counseling Psychologists?

Clinical or counseling psychology is delivered by someone who is trained in those branches of psychology and who may be a licensed psychologist. Typically, they specialize in specific emotional or personality-disorder problems (e.g., eating disorders), and they treat all kinds of patients, including athletes. The athletic experience can be very stressful to some athletes, and it can negatively affect their performance or their ability to function as healthy people. A sport psychologist may recognize symptoms in an athlete that could result in a referral to a clinical or counseling psychologist. Part of helping athletes reach their fullest potential includes knowing when to provide alternative resources and referrals.

What Does Mind-Body Conditioning Have to Offer Figure Skaters?

Given the description of what mind-body conditioning is, it should be clear why this integrated approach is important. However, this additional aspect is something that you may not have considered: Figure skating is a fun and rewarding sport, but it takes years of practice to improve skills. Because this sport requires so much learning, some terrific skaters may become frustrated and quit the sport prematurely.

Mind-body conditioning skills apply to practice as well as competitive performance. Many of the things you will learn in this book are intended to be applied and practiced during your skating practice sessions. Practicing psychological skills in conjunction with practicing physical skills not only helps you master the psychological skill in the ideal setting, but also makes practice time more interesting and enjoyable.

How Does Motivation Relate to Mind-Body Conditioning?

You recognize how important practice is in the sport of figure skating, and you know how much time you spend doing it. The training and preparation habits of all great performers can be traced to a combination of physical ability and a drive to be the very best. What is it that motivates someone to spend so much time working to accomplish a goal? For some reason, or reasons, you come to believe that the goal is worth spending a lifetime (and large amounts of money) to achieve.

Many different things can motivate you. Sometimes motivation is inside you, and it comes from a personal desire to find success without outside rewards and enticements. Sometimes, you may be motivated by outside factors such as a desire to gain fame or fortune. Motivation to achieve success in sport is not simply an inborn instinct that everyone possesses like the drive to eat or drink when hungry or thirsty. Instead, it is something that is learned and can be developed. The word motivation comes from the Latin word *movere*, which means "to move." The desire to move and change, as opposed to remaining the same, is the essence of motivation. This idea is really an oversimplified way of thinking about motivation. Usually, motivation is more complex and specific to a given situation. Understanding your own level of motivation and commitment to figure skating can help you to develop both, which will allow you to get more out of your sport should you choose to do so.

In closing, you must understand the importance of practice and training to prepare for being your best. As you learn these new psychological skills, you must be equally committed to practicing them. Just like your physical skills, your psychological skills only help you if they are well rehearsed and ready when it is time to compete.

Application Exercises

Exercise 1: Introduction to Journaling

Keeping a mind-body conditioning journal is an important part of implementing the kind of training discussed in this book. As you will see, journaling has many benefits, including helping you on those days when you feel less motivated than usual. Your journal might be in book form, in digital audio form, or even an online blog. Choose the medium that works best for you and your lifestyle.

For your first journal entry, describe how you got started in skating. What prompted you to begin? Then, move on to describe what you enjoy about skating now. Be as descriptive as possible, writing in a way that makes sense to you. Finish by describing why you want to become a better skater and how you think this book will help you in doing so.

Exercise 2: Dare to Dream

Successful performers often admit that they had a vision of their future success. To be a successful athlete, it is helpful to dream big but to have a sense of how you will fulfill your dream as well. In your journal, address each of the following steps to discover your potential skating destiny.

Step 1: What's in Store for Me?

When you look into the future a few months, a year, five years, and 10 years, what role does figure skating hold for you? Where do you see yourself at each of those different times? What level of skater do you expect to be? Do you think you will still be skating? How might skating be different for you at each of those times? Don't judge yourself…just let your honest thoughts flow.

Step 2: Reality Check

Now, reflect back on what you wrote. Are you being realistic? If you know that you are, then start to consider where you see yourself at those times compared to where you are right now. What are the differences between yourself now and how you see yourself at those different times?

Step 3: How I'll Get There

Now, think about what you might have had to do to get to where you see yourself at those future times. What did you spend your time doing? What could you have done instead? What sacrifices did you need to make? If you chose skating over other things, why do you think you did that? What motivated you?

This journal exercise is an important step to complete to begin to realize your potential. Reflecting on your journal entries following tough practices or competitions may lift your spirits. It may also serve as a reminder of your initial experiences with mind-body conditioning, and how developing these skills will help you not only in your sport, but also in life in general.

2

The Inner Circle

In the journaling exercises in the last chapter, you may have discovered some things about yourself and those around you who support you in your figure skating efforts. To become the very best you can be, you do need to be focused on yourself and what you are trying to accomplish. At the same time, you also should acknowledge and appreciate those people who help you develop as an athlete and a person. The relationships you develop as a result of your sport can get you through rough times, but these relationships also can be significant sources of stress. In this chapter, you will learn about your *inner circle*—the people who have the most significant impact on your skating—and how to foster these relationships, build harmony, and avoid common pitfalls among its members.

In sports like figure skating where athletic development may start at a very young age, the inner circle will typically consist of you, your primary coach, and one or both of your parents. The inner circle is a natural aspect of all sports involving young people, and how well you all get along is very important for your success. Parents are often heavily involved in figure skating—in some ways that are productive and in others that may have a negative effect.

Even if you compete at a high level, everyone in the inner circle needs to enter the relationship with the understanding that skating has many benefits beyond winning competitions. Learning to skate involves mastering challenging motor skills, which also happens to improve your physical health and fitness. Skating also can teach you self-discipline, respect for authority, competitiveness, cooperativeness, sportsmanship, and self-confidence. In addition, skating can be viewed as an important social activity where you make new friends and become part of an even bigger skating community. And, of course, skating is (or should be) just plain fun.

The Center of the Inner Circle—You

How you train as a figure skater ultimately should be *your* decision and should emphasize *you* as the center of the inner circle. As the center, it is your responsibility to speak up for yourself when you feel yourself shifting away from the center of your inner circle. For example, the other members of your inner circle may need to be reminded about the fun factor involved in skating. One of the fastest ways to destroy that fun factor is when you, your coach, or your parent start approaching skating as though it is your job. Skating is, first and foremost, a play activity, and you deserve to enjoy skating in your own way. It is important that your skating program keeps you at the center and is not dominated by the adults in the inner circle.

You know that the adults in your inner circle are overly involved with your skating when their influence starts to make you feel unusually stressed. Sometimes parents and coaches try to live their dreams through you, their child/skater, which can make you feel like you have to win and achieve in order to gain their love and approval.

If this situation applies to you, you can explain that placing excessive pressure on you decreases both the fun factor and the potential for personal growth. Impress upon your parents (and coach if necessary) that your figure skating is for you and *not* for the adults in your inner circle. To foster a healthy relationship between the adults in the inner circle, your coach and parents must be willing to:

- Share you, the skater
- Accept your disappointments
- Model good sportsmanship
- Give you time
- Let you make your own decisions

Share You, the Skater

When you begin working with a coach, your parents are putting you in your coach's care and trusting your coach to guide your skating experience. Doing so involves your parents accepting your coach's authority. Your parents also need to accept the fact that you may develop strong feelings of admiration and affection for your coach. This situation can be tough on some parents, especially if prior to becoming involved in skating all that affection and admiration was directed solely at them. Enlisting the help of a coach does not mean that your parents cannot have any input, but when it comes to your skating training, your coach is the boss.

Accept Your Disappointments

The testing and competitions involved in figure skating allows every skater to experience the thrill of victory and the agony of defeat. Your coach and your parents need to be there for you not only to enjoy your victories, but also to provide support when you are disappointed and hurt. Neither your coach nor your parents should be embarrassed, ashamed, or angry if, for example, you cry after experiencing a defeat. Instead, they should help you learn from the experience. Doing so, without denying the validity of your feelings, can help you see the positive side of the situation and help you change those feelings of disappointment into self-acceptance.

Model Good Sportsmanship

Parents and coaches may need to be reminded that they are important role models for your behavior. It is not surprising that parents and coaches who lose control of themselves often produce skaters who are prone to emotional outbursts and poor self-discipline. You can hardly be expected to learn good sportsmanship and self-control if your coach or your parents lack these qualities.

Give You Time

Figure skating requires a significant amount of time to learn and to practice. Your coach and your parents need to decide how much time they can realistically devote to your figure skating training. Conflicts arise when parents and coaches are very busy, but also very interested and want to encourage you. The people in your inner circle need to communicate honestly about time commitments, and they should not promise more time than they can actually deliver. Talk with your parents about your skating experiences, and encourage them to make every effort to watch some of your performances and competitions.

Let You Make Your Own Decisions

Accepting responsibility for your own behavior and decisions is an essential part of growing up. Parents and coaches may have ambitions for you, but they cannot dominate your life. Be sure to hear them out when they offer suggestions and guidance about skating, but ultimately and within reasonable limits, they should let you go your own way. Skating can offer your parents an introduction to the major parental challenge of letting go.

Inner Circle Harmony: Communication

Your parents have both the right and the responsibility to ask questions about how you are spending your time during your skating training sessions. Your coach should be willing to answer questions and be open to your parents' input. Communication needs to work both ways. If your coach can keep the lines of communication open, your coach will be more likely to have a constructive relationship with your parents.

Open communication does not give your parents permission to be disrespectful toward your coach. Instead, it is an opportunity for your parents to express their genuine concerns, and they should be able to trust that your coach will listen openly. Your parents need to understand the proper time and place for parent-coach conversations. That time is not during practice or competition, and it is never in front of you without your permission. Your coach should take the lead in telling your parents what times and places are best suited for these types of discussions.

Open communication can be challenged when disagreements occur. Parents and coaches often tend to disagree when it comes to their opinions about your abilities. This differing of opinions is one of several reasons why it is valuable to use a performance assessment system to provide you and the rest of your inner circle with objective feedback on your skating progress. (You will learn how to create and implement such a system in this book.) Even when performance data is readily available and you are demonstrating growth, sometimes parents will disagree with what coaches are doing.

As your inner circle members, parents and coaches need to listen to each other and evaluate each other's messages, even if they do not agree. Parents need to realize that your coach is the professional and that no coach can please everyone. No one can ask any more of you than what your coach should be asking of you—do the very best you can, and always look for ways to improve.

The Pitfalls: Common Parent Problems

While you can always replace a coach who doesn't work out, your parents will always be your parents. As the center of the circle, you need to be aware that your parents are probably really enthusiastic and have a genuine concern for you and your well-being. If and when they do cause problems for you about skating, they may not even realize that they are doing so. Instead of getting angry with them, you and your coach should point out, as nicely as possible, how they are negatively affecting your skating. Some common parent problems include:

- Showing disinterest
- Being overly critical
- Being overly protective
- Being a sideline coach

Showing Disinterest

The most noticeable characteristic of disinterested parents is that they are not around. If this situation applies to you, you may find it upsetting that your parents aren't there to watch you test, perform, or compete. As key members of the inner circle, you and your coach should find out why your parents are not more involved, and let them know that their involvement is welcome.

Avoid judging your parents. Many possible reasons could be causing them to miss your events, including, for example, having to be at work to pay for skating. Everyone in the inner circle should understand that one of the benefits of figure skating is that it can draw you and your parents closer together by providing your parents with a new interest in the form of your sport. If you feel that your parents are too disinterested in your skating, you may need help too. You may start to feel insecure about why your parents are not showing interest, which may lead to acting out to get negative attention in attempts to "make" your parents notice you. A good coach should notice and take action if parents appear disinterested, especially if it begins to impact your skating experiences. Your coach should encourage you and show an interest in you as a person, not just as a skater.

Being Overly Critical

You know your parents are overly critical when they consistently scold you and put you down. It's as though they are never quite satisfied with your performance. Parents who come across this way are too involved and can take the fun out of your skating. They may need to be reminded that it is you who is at the center of the inner circle when it comes to skating.

Again, try not to judge your parents. You are their child, and sometimes it is hard for them *not* to relate your successes and disappointments to their own. As a result, they may be too hard on you. If this situation applies to you, you or your coach should attempt to make your parents aware of this problem as tactfully as possible. Explain how constant criticism makes you upset and causes you stress, which makes it harder to improve. Encourage them to use praise and encouragement instead because doing so has both instructional and motivational value and may help you improve more quickly.

Being Overly Protective

Overprotective parents usually look troubled and make worrisome comments whenever you are practicing, performing, or competing. You know your parents are overprotective if they frequently threaten to remove you from the sport because of the dangers involved in figure skating.

You and your coach should try to eliminate the fear of injury by reassuring your parents that skating is fairly safe, especially as your skills improve. Have your coach talk with your parents about protective equipment and off-ice conditioning for injury prevention. Your coach also may point out how good coaching and program administration add to the safety of figure skating.

Being a Sideline Coach

When your parents make suggestions to you as you are skating and about your skating when you are off the ice, chances are they suffer from being a sideline coach. Even if one or both of your parents previously skated competitively, you now have a professional coach who is being paid to teach you how to skate. The problem with parents who are sideline coaches is that they may contradict your real coach's instructions and disrupt your learning process.

If your parent is a sideline coach, the following steps may help you solve this problem. First, give your coach your full attention during lessons, and follow her instructions as closely as possible. Describe the problem to her, and decide if it makes sense for you or her to talk with your parent. Explain to your "sideline-coach parent" that listening to instructions from people other than your coach is confusing to you. Your coach should tell your parent privately how confusing it is for you when two or more people are telling you what to do. To make things easier on you, your coach may ask your parent to be either a full-time assistant coach or a full-time cheerleader, whichever role makes the most sense given your parent's skills in figure skating instruction.

To summarize, the relationships between the inner circle members (i.e., you as the skater, your coach, and your parents) impact your ability to be the best you can be as a figure skater. Awareness of the health of these relationships and open communication are key to ensuring that the inner circle supports rather than negatively impacts your skating experiences.

Application Exercise

Exercise 1: Examine Your Inner Circle

In your journal, describe your inner circle. Who is in your inner circle? Have members of your inner circle changed over the course of your skating experiences? How is communication between the members of the inner circle? Do any areas need improvement? Do your parents suffer from any of the parent problems described in this chapter? If so, what steps are you or your coach taking to address these problems?

3

Pre-Season Assessment

To set effective and realistic goals for your skating season, you need to have some idea of your current level of proficiency. Begin your season by sitting down with your inner circle and taking a comprehensive look at where you are right now and what you should focus on as you train for your competitive season. When you use a mind-body conditioning approach, your body helps train your mind, and your mind helps train your body, so your pre-season assessment should include examining your technical skills, physical fitness, psychological skills, and presentation skills. In this chapter, you'll learn about how to assess each of these areas.

Keep in mind, figure skating is a sport that is scored both objectively and subjectively. Some aspects of your skating can be evaluated objectively, such as your level of physical fitness. Other aspects, such as your presentation and, to some degree, your psychological training skills, are evaluated more subjectively. Even though objectivity is more fact-based and subjectivity more opinion-based, all constructive feedback is helpful when developing an effective, holistic training program for skating.

Technical Skills

Your technical skills are best assessed by your coach and other skating technical specialists. Recent testing and competition results can also give you some indication of your technical proficiency. Be sure to evaluate your skills in all elements of skating (e.g., jumps, spins, footwork), on their own as well as in programs. If possible, use your organization's scoring system for your level as your guideline. In the Application Exercises at the end of this chapter, a specific guideline is provided to help you get an assessment of these skills from your coach and others.

Physical Fitness

To be a successful athlete, you need to be in great physical condition. In the United States and other countries, physical appearance is often confused with physical fitness. You can be very lean and look attractive and yet be deconditioned. Simply participating in a sport, even an intense one like figure skating, may not make you physically fit. To perform at your best, you need to be as fit and healthy as possible. Fitness, as defined by the American College of Sports Medicine and other health and fitness certifying bodies, includes cardiorespiratory fitness, muscular strength, muscular endurance, flexibility, and body composition.

Cardiorespiratory fitness refers to the ability of the body's cells to uptake and use oxygen efficiently. Also referred to as cardiovascular fitness, this component of physical fitness impacts your ability to exert more effort while skating, without becoming unduly fatigued. Skaters need to develop well-trained aerobic (steady-state) and anaerobic (high intensity) cardio systems to be successful in practice and in competition.

Muscular strength refers to the maximal force you can exert, whereas *muscular endurance* refers to being able to perform an action repeatedly. All aspects of skating rely on muscular endurance, and jumps and lifts in particular rely on muscular strength. Developing muscular strength and endurance is also helpful for injury prevention.

Flexibility refers to the ability to extend or lengthen muscles through joint action, and it is of particular importance in this sport due to the emphasis on extension of the body. *Body composition* refers to how body weight is distributed, and it is usually expressed as a percent of lean body mass versus a percent of fat mass.

A thorough pre-season assessment includes collecting a baseline measurement in these five areas of fitness. In addition, other sport-specific skills such as balance, power, and agility should be assessed. Carl Poe, a leading authority on physical conditioning for figure skating, has written a comprehensive text that includes assessments and sample programs appropriate for skaters at different levels (*Conditioning for Figure Skating: Off-Ice Techniques for On-Ice Performance*, 2002). The USFS website also supplies sample exercise programs for skaters at different levels to help them improve in these areas of fitness. A physical pre-season assessment is included in the Application Exercises at the end of this chapter. After collecting baseline data, plan to reassess every six to eight weeks throughout the season and make modifications to your training program based in part on the results of these reassessments. As all serious skaters should do, you should follow this procedure—a practice known as *periodization*—to ensure you are making progress in your fitness levels, which, in turn, will enhance your skating skills.

To perform at your best level in figure skating, you must be well trained physically. If you are not well trained physically, no amount of talent or psychological skills training will make you successful. Your physical training and technique, when well practiced, will enhance your psychological readiness and vice versa. This is the heart of mind-body conditioning.

Psychological Skills

Garry Martin is a Canadian sport psychologist who has worked extensively with figure skaters in that country. During his first few years of providing psychological skills training for figure skaters, he kept track of the areas in which skaters requested help for improving performance at practices and competitions. He used that information to develop a pre-season questionnaire for skaters (Martin, 1998), which is included in the Application Exercises at the end of this chapter. The questionnaire is one method that you can use to determine which areas of psychological skills training you would like to or need to improve to enhance your skating performance.

Another way that psychological skills are often assessed is through a technique called *performance profiling*. With this approach, you make up the assessment and then rate yourself based on your findings. Your coach should also rate you on the same constructs. The result is a performance profile (Figure 3-1), which you can then use to set goals for the specific psychological skills you'd like to improve. More information and directions for how to complete a performance profile can be found in the Application Exercises at the end of this chapter.

Construct	I	ISA	SSA	(ISA–SSA)	Discrepancy (ISA–SSA) x I
Good and focused	10	10	7	3	30
Willing to do what it takes	9	10	7	3	27
Good attitude	10	10	10	0	0
Come with a plan	9	10	9	1	9
Disciplined	10	10	8	2	20
Handling negative critiquing well	10	10	7	3	30
Being able to bounce back	9	10	8	2	18
Love of skating	10	10	10	0	0
Handle pressure well consistently	10	10	7	3	30
Strong self-belief	10	10	9	1	10

I = Perceived importance
ISA = Ideal self-assessment
SSA = Subject self-assessment

Figure 3-1. Sample performance profile: psychological skills for figure skating

You might find that you prefer one method of psychological skills assessment over the other. Feel free to use the questionnaire, the performance profile, or both to determine which psychological skills you'd like to focus on for the upcoming competitive season.

Presentation Skills

Martin (1998) also has designed an assessment that examines presentation during program run-throughs. He noticed that when young skaters do program run-throughs at practice, they tend to try to perform all of their elements, but they do not practice their presentation. During program run-throughs, he noted things such as skaters tugging on their costumes, flipping their hair out of their faces, frowning or making a face when they miss an element, scratching themselves, wiping their noses, and so on. If these things are occurring during practice, they may accidentally happen during competition. You are not truly practicing a run-through if your presentation is not the same as what you would want it to be in competition. Martin suggests that you score your presentation during a run-through using a rating system. Having a pre-season presentation rating will give you some idea as to which areas may require some improvement. Martin's rating system is included in the Application Exercises at the end of this chapter.

You can also use performance profiling to assess your presentation skills. If possible, watch a video from a recent practice run-through. It's hard to evaluate yourself by recall or when you're sensitive to the fact that you're observing your own presentation skills. Be sure to have your inner circle evaluate your presentation skills as well, using the constructs that you choose. This activity is also included in the Application Exercises.

In summary, an effective pre-season assessment involves getting a comprehensive picture of all the aspects that affect your skating performance, including technical skills, physical fitness, psychological skills, and presentation skills. Learning your strengths and areas that need improvement can help you set goals, stay motivated, develop a smarter training program, and use your training time more effectively. When taken together, all of these actions result in performance enhancement.

Application Exercises

To create your own comprehensive pre-season assessment, you will want to complete the following exercises. In some cases, you may choose to complete more than one type of assessment. The objective is to gather enough information to design an effective, motivating training program that will enable you to be the very best you can be.

Exercise 1: Technical Skills Assessment

Create a three-column table in your journal entitled "Pre-Season Technical Skills Assessment" (Figure 3-2). Be sure to include the date of the assessment and who is evaluating your skills. In the first column, list all the elements you do in your program (or programs) and any other elements you are currently developing. Have your coach score each element according to USFS standards when presented by itself as well as when skated in a program. Be sure to include enough rows for all of your elements, including steps and other footwork.

Date: _____ Evaluator: _____		
Element	**By Itself**	**In Program**

Figure 3-2. Sample pre-season technical skills assessment

Exercise 2: Physical Fitness Assessment

The physical fitness assessment shown in Figure 3-3 is best administered by a qualified strength and conditioning specialist (NSCA-CSCS). For further explanations on how to conduct these assessments and additional testing information, see *Conditioning for Figure Skating: Off-Ice Techniques for On-Ice Performance* (Poe, 2002).

Exercise 3a: Psychological Skills Assessment—Martin's Mental Skills Questionnaire for Skaters

Using Martin's questionnaire is one method for evaluating your psychological skills (Figure 3-4). Choose this option or feel free to skip to the performance profile method (Exercise 3b).

Resting Measurements

Heart rate: _____   Blood pressure: _____

Height: _____   Weight: _____

Body composition: _____

Aerobic/Anaerobic Systems

On-ice power stroking heart rate: _____

On-ice long program heart rate: _____

Three-minute step test: _____

Power

Medicine ball shot: _____   Double-leg vertical jump: _____

Single-leg vertical jump (right leg): _____

Single-leg vertical jump (left leg):   _____

Strength/Endurance

5 RM bench press: _____   5 RM back squat: _____

Pull-ups: _____   Push-ups: _____

Crunches: _____

Flexibility

Sit and reach: _____   Spinal flexion: _____

Spinal extension: _____

Lateral spinal flexion (right):_____   Lateral spinal flexion (left): _____

Hip flexion (right): _____   Hip flexion (left): _____

Hip extension (right): _____   Hip extension (left): _____

Knee flexion (right): _____   Knee flexion (left): _____

Knee extension (right): _____   Knee extension (left): _____

Ankle dorsiflexion (right): _____   Ankle dorsiflexion (left): _____

Ankle plantar flexion (right): _____   Ankle plantar flexion (left): _____

Balance

Right leg: _____

Left leg: _____

Figure 3-3. Sample physical fitness assessment for figure skating

For each of the following, answer the question: Would you say you need to improve this skill?	Not Sure	Definitely No		To Some Extent		Definitely Yes
<u>Regarding Practices</u> 1. Set specific goals for every practice		1	2	3	4	5
2. Arrive at every practice totally committed to doing your best		1	2	3	4	5
3. Consistently be stretched and warmed up before stepping on the ice at practice		1	2	3	4	5
4. Be more focused when doing your elements		1	2	3	4	5
5. Stay positive and not get down on yourself when you're having a bad practice		1	2	3	4	5
6. Make better use of full practice time		1	2	3	4	5
7. Overcome fear of doing difficult elements		1	2	3	4	5
8. Improve consistency of elements you can already do		1	2	3	4	5
9. Feel more confident about your ability to do difficult elements		1	2	3	4	5
10. Not worry about what other skaters are doing		1	2	3	4	5
11. Figure out how to monitor progress on a new element that you are learning so that you don't get discouraged when progress seems slow		1	2	3	4	5
12. Do more complete program run-throughs (and try everything in your program)		1	2	3	4	5

Adapted from Martin, 1998

Figure 3-4. Martin's mental skills questionnaire for skaters

For each of the following, answer the question: Would you say you need to improve this skill?	Not Sure	Definitely No		To Some Extent		Definitely Yes
13. Keep track of your percent landed during program run-throughs		1	2	3	4	5
14. Score your presentation during program run-through		1	2	3	4	5
15. Make better use of mental imagery to improve your elements		1	2	3	4	5
16. Make better use of key words for elements		1	2	3	4	5
17. Practice more positive self-talk during program run-throughs		1	2	3	4	5
18. Keep a written record of your progress in meeting your goals		1	2	3	4	5
Regarding Competitions 1. Stay confident at practices when you see what the other skaters are doing		1	2	3	4	5
2. At practices, forget about other skaters and just focus on your own skating		1	2	3	4	5
3. Avoid putting excess pressure on yourself when you see what other skaters are doing at practices		1	2	3	4	5
4. Learn how not to worry about other skaters		1	2	3	4	5
5. Learn how not to worry about where you will place		1	2	3	4	5
6. Have a better time-management plan for the entire competition so that you are well organized, eat healthy, and get lots of restte as		1	2	3	4	5

Figure 3-4. Martin's mental skills questionnaire for skaters (cont.)

For each of the following, answer the question: Would you say you need to improve this skill?	Not Sure	Definitely No		To Some Extent		Definitely Yes
7. Skate as well during a competition as during the last two or three weeks before competition (up to your potential)		1	2	3	4	5
8. Stay loose (not too tense) during the last half hour before the warm-up		1	2	3	4	5
9. Stay loose (not too tense) during the warm-up		1	2	3	4	5
10. Stay loose (not too tense) during the last half hour after the warm-up while waiting your turn		1	2	3	4	5
11. Stay loose (not too tense) when you go on the ice for your turn		1	2	3	4	5
12. Feel confident about your skating while stretching before the warm-up		1	2	3	4	5
13. Not be psyched out by other skaters		1	2	3	4	5
14. Feel confident about your skating during the warm-up		1	2	3	4	5
15. Feel confident about your skating after the warm-up, while waiting your turn to skate		1	2	3	4	5
16. Take it one element at a time during your program (not getting ahead of yourself or thinking only about hard elements)		1	2	3	4	5
17. Concentrate on the easy elements as well as the hard ones		1	2	3	4	5
18. Stay positive and skate well for the rest of your program, even if you fall		1	2	3	4	5

Figure 3-4. Martin's mental skills questionnaire for skaters (cont.)

Exercise 3b: Psychological Skills Assessment—Performance Profile

The process of creating a performance profile consists of the following three steps.

Step 1: Identify the Constructs

Consider this question: What are the key psychological factors or characteristics of elite-level figure skaters? Take some time to think about your answer, and then list 10 to 15 of these factors or characteristics (referred to as *constructs*) on the psychological skills performance profile template (Figure 3-5).

Step 2: Self-Assessment

On a scale of 0 (being not at all important) to 10 (being extremely important), rate how important (abbreviated as I) you think each construct is for an elite-level figure skater. Be specific—different sports place different demands on athletes.

Next, use the same 0 to 10 scale to rate your current perceptions of yourself (subject self-assessment or SSA) in relation to an ideal state of 10 (ideal self-assessment or ISA). Subtract the SSA from the ISA and multiply by the I number to find the discrepancy score. Higher discrepancies indicate areas that may need to be addressed through training.

Construct	I	ISA	SSA	(ISA–SSA)	Discrepancy (ISA–SSA) x I

I = Perceived importance
ISA = Ideal self-assessment
SSA = Subject self-assessment

Figure 3-5. Psychological skills performance profile template

Step 3: Coach's Assessment

Have your coach assess you on these same constructs. This process will help you determine if you and your coach are in agreement over the relevant constructs. The coach-skater relationship is much stronger when vision, goals, and targets are shared and agreed upon. Difficulties can arise when the opposite is true.

Exercise 4a: Presentation Skills Assessment—Martin's Rating Scale

As with psychological skills, you have two choices for assessing presentation skills. You may choose to complete one or both assessments. The first option is Martin's rating scale. Have someone watch you skate your program during practice when you don't know that person is there. As this person watches you, he should evaluate your presentation skills and score each of the items listed (Figure 3-6). The first four items must reflect the character, mood, and beat of the music (i.e., crisp and forceful in some places, slow and dramatic in others, often exaggerated, and always expressive).

For the first four items listed, score as follows:

2   = Excellent, very expressive, and appropriate
1.5 = Generally very good
1   = Room for improvement
0.5 = Definite room for improvement
0   = Poor

For lack of negatives, score as follows:
2   = No negatives (such as skater playing with hair, scratching nose, tugging on outfit, etc.)
1   = One negative
0   = More than one negative

Presentation Skill	Pre-Season Rating
Head movements crisp and/or expressive to the music	
Shoulder and body movements appropriately expressive to the music	
Hand and arm movements crisp and/or expressive to the music	
Appropriate facial expression and/or smiles in the direction of the judges' area	
Lack of negatives	
Total (10 max.)	

Figure 3-6. Martin's presentation skills assessment

Exercise 4b: Presentation Skills Assessment—Performance Profile

For this exercise (Figure 3-7), follow the same steps used when creating a performance profile for psychological skills, but develop constructs based on the following question: What are the key presentation characteristics or behaviors exhibited by top figure skaters when they skate their programs?

Construct	I	ISA	SSA	(ISA–SSA)	Discrepancy (ISA–SSA) x I
I = Perceived importance ISA = Ideal self-assessment SSA = Subject self-assessment					

Figure 3-7. Presentation skills performance profile template

4

Seasonal Goal Setting

In the last chapter, you learned how to complete a comprehensive pre-season assessment. The results from this assessment can help you to set goals for the competitive season. In this chapter, you'll explore ways to help you set these goals effectively. First, you'll learn why goal setting at the beginning of the season is an important exercise. Next, you'll examine different types of goals and look at what makes goals effective. The Application Exercises at the end of this chapter will help you create seasonal goals that are appropriate for you.

Why Set Goals?

Research shows that top athletes set both long- and short-term goals. Goal setting defines your dreams, and goals can be a powerful motivational tool to improve performance. Proper goal setting can help you focus your attention, guide your actions, and maximize your potential. Perhaps most importantly, setting and meeting goals is fun and personally satisfying. How you feel about yourself—your feelings of self-worth or self-esteem—is important. Setting and meeting goals can be a rewarding experience, which helps you feel good about yourself and be your best.

Setting goals at the beginning of your competitive season also gives your training program more direction and purpose. If you know what you are setting out to achieve, you have a much better chance of accomplishing it.

Types of Goals

Sport psychologists have categorized goals into different types. If you are familiar with these different types of goals before you begin goal setting, you will be able to tell the difference between goals that are effective versus goals that are not.

Subjective goals include things like having fun, getting in better shape, and trying your best. You have an idea about what they mean, but it might be hard to tell when you've achieved them.

General objective goals are the types of goals that you can tell that they happened, but you may not necessarily be sure how or why they happened. Some examples of general objective goals are winning a competition or making a skating team.

Specific objective goals are the types of goals that you can pinpoint exactly how and why they happened. Some examples of this type of goal include increasing the number of flip jumps landed during a practice session or decreasing traveling during a combination spin.

In addition to categorizing goals as subjective or objective and as general or specific, goals can be categorized based on the standard of comparison. *Outcome goals* involve comparisons between you and other competitors. An example of an outcome goal is placing higher than another skater at a regional competition. In contrast, *performance goals* focus on your own personal improvements over past performances. Setting the goal of improving your personal best score for your short program is an example of a performance goal. *Process goals* specify how performance goals are achieved—in other words, what you will be doing during performance (e.g., consistently pulling in tight during your air ride in your jumps, staying centered over the ball of your foot during spins, and so on).

So, why should you care about these different types of goals? Certain types of goals are more useful in enhancing performance than other types of goals, so it makes sense for you to focus on creating effective goals when setting seasonal goals as well as when setting short-term goals.

SMART Goal Setting

Research has shown that the goals that are most effective can be summarized by using the acronym SMART:

Specific
Measurable
Attainable
Realistic
Timely

Specific means that your goals should be straight-forward, and they should emphasize what you want to happen. Specifics help you to focus your efforts and clearly define what you are going to do. You are being specific when you can identify the what, why, how, and when of the goal. What are you going to do? Use action words (verbs) to begin your goal, such as *"increase* the height of my Axel," or *"compete* in two out-of-state competitions." *Why* is this goal important at this time? *What* do you ultimately want to accomplish? *How* are you going to do it? By *when*? An example of a specific goal would be "increase the height of my Axel (*what*) by completing off-ice plyometric exercises twice weekly (*how*) so I can begin to practice a double Axel (*why*) by June 1 (*when*)."

Make the goals you set very specific, clear, and easy. Instead of setting a goal to do better at your next competition, set a specific goal to improve your program score by achieving higher grades of execution on your spins, for example.

If you can't measure something, you can't manage it. Choose goals with *measurable* progress so you can see changes occur. How will you know when you reach your goal? Be specific. Saying "I want to improve my program score by 10 points in my next competition" describes the specific target to be measured. Saying "I want to be a good skater" is not as measurable. Be sure to establish concrete guidelines for measuring progress toward the attainment of each goal you set. When you measure your progress, you stay on track, you reach your target dates, and you experience the thrill of achievement that encourages you to continue setting and reaching new goals.

When you identify goals that are most important to you, you begin to figure out ways you can make them come true. You develop the attitudes, abilities, and skills to *attain* them. You begin to realize that goals that once seemed out of your reach may actually be attainable. However, if you set goals that are too far out of your reach, you probably won't commit to following through and taking action toward meeting the goal. Although you may start with the best intentions, deep inside you are reminded that it's too much for you, which will stop you from even giving it your best. A goal needs to stretch you slightly so you feel you can accomplish it if you commit to it. For example, if you set a goal to lose 20 pounds in one week, you are setting yourself up for failure. But setting a goal to lose just one pound, and when you've achieved that, aiming to lose another pound, will keep it achievable for you. Meeting goals helps you feel successful and keeps you motivated.

Realistic does not mean "easy." It means "doable." It means that the goal might be moderately difficult, but it is still within your ability. Moderately difficult goals seem to lead to the best performance so that they challenge, but do not overwhelm, you. Being realistic also involves devising a plan or a way of getting there. The goal needs to be realistic for you and where you are at the moment. A goal of never falling again on a jump is not realistic for any skater. However, it may be more realistic to set a goal of having a smaller percent of falls during jump attempts. You can then choose to work toward gradually reducing the number of falls you allow yourself, and decide when this goal feels realistic for you to attain. Be sure to set goals that require a reasonable amount of effort to attain. If you make them too difficult, you set the stage for failure, but setting them too low sends the message that you aren't very capable. Set the bar high enough for a satisfying achievement.

And finally, your goals should be *timely*. Set a time frame for accomplishing the goal (e.g., by next week, in three months, by next season). Putting an ending point on your goal gives you a clear target date to work toward. If you don't set a time, the commitment is too vague. It tends not to happen because you feel you can start at any time. Without a time limit, there's no urgency to start taking action now. But make sure that the time that you set is measurable, attainable, and realistic.

Now you should have a better understanding of the different types of goals and the goal-setting practices (SMART) that lead to effective performance. Go ahead and complete the Application Exercises to set your goals for the season.

Application Exercises

Exercise 1: Desire-Based Goal Setting

Think about your future goals for figure skating. In your journal, write the heading: Desire-Based Goal Setting. Then, keeping in mind that at this point, it is more important to get your ideas down on paper than to make these SMART goals, complete the following sentences:
- My dream goals for figure skating in the next few years are…
- My element/program goals for the coming season are…
- My competition goals for this season include…

Exercise 2: Performance-Based Goal Setting

Now, review the pre-season performance assessment you completed in the last chapter. In your journal, write the heading: Performance-Based Goal Setting. Then, without worrying about making these SMART goals, complete the following sentences:
- Based on the assessment of my technical skills, my goals in this area include…
- Based on the assessment of my physical fitness, my goals in this area include…
- Based on the assessment of my psychological skills, my goals in this area include…
- Based on the assessment of my presentation skills, my goals in this area include…

Exercise 3: Goals for This Competitive Season

Review the two lists of goals that you created when completing the first two exercises. Is there overlap? Label the goals as outcome, performance, or process goals. Then, from these two lists, create your final list of goals for the season. Be sure to keep the number of outcome and performance goals manageable. Having too many seasonal goals makes monitoring progress a chore and less motivating. Keep in mind that your goals for your physical fitness, psychological skills, and presentation skills are likely process goals that support your goals for your technical skills as well as for some of your desired seasonal goals. After you've created your list, check them against the SMART guidelines. Are they specific? Measurable? Attainable? Realistic? Timely? Confirm your goals with your inner circle, and then commit to them by putting them on a calendar that you and others will see often.

5

Productive Practice

An old joke exists about a tourist who asks a New Yorker, "Pardon me sir, but how do I get to Carnegie Hall?" The man replies, "Practice, practice, practice." To become really good at anything, you need to practice…a lot. Spending a great deal of time practicing skating elements can be both physically and psychologically fatiguing. In this chapter, you'll learn specific psychological skills and strategies that you can use to develop your practice sessions, making them more productive, effective, and enjoyable. Some of these skills will be familiar to you. For example, you have already learned about seasonal goal setting in the previous chapter. In this chapter, you'll learn how to apply those same skills and set specific goals for practice sessions.

You also will be introduced to some new skills in this chapter. These new skills will be applied to improving the quality of your practice sessions. In later chapters, some of the skills will be revisited, and you will learn other ways the skills and techniques can be used to help you both in practice and in competition. For example, this chapter introduces imagery, the psychological skill that allows you to create vivid images in your mind. You will learn how to assess your current imagery skills, and then develop them so that you can use imagery to get more out of your practice sessions. You'll also learn some planning and self-monitoring skills that will help you improve how quickly you learn and develop your skills.

Goal Setting and Practice Planning

Most of the goals you set for practice sessions are process goals that will help you meet your seasonal goals. As such, they will be very specific. You've learned that objective goals, such as increasing the number of repetitions practiced for a specific element, are easier to measure than subjective goals. However, subjectivity is a part of figure skating, and one very important aspect—quality—is, in fact, a subjective measure.

You want to put in quality practice sessions when you are at the rink. To know that you are making improvements, you need to be able to measure the quality of your skating elements, which you can do by using a rating scale. Define what constitutes high quality for the various elements that you practice. You may choose to use your club's rating system or your own. For example, on a scale of 1 to 10, you might decide that a 9-quality camel spin is defined as "almost perfect—centered, fast, with strong extension and body position."

Set specific goals for what you want to accomplish at every practice. Include quality as well as quantity. For example, "land at least four double-flip/double-loop combination jumps (*quantity*) with a rating of 8 or better (*quality*)." You can use your journal to keep a written record of your goals so that you can monitor your progress and stay motivated.

Think about your practice goals as your plan for practice. Your practice plan should list not only the elements that you want to practice during your session, but also your goals in terms of number of repetitions and the quality of execution (e.g., a minimum of eight attempts at the triple loop with a quality rating of 7 or better). Research shows that, during a 45-minute freestyle session, a hardworking novice single skater will have between 55 and 70 good attempts at jumps and spins (counting elements during the warm-up and both inside and outside of program run-throughs). As competitions draw near, you should be practicing segments of your programs and doing simulations of competition run-throughs. Set goals for those run-throughs as well.

Focus—Developing Awareness and Mindfulness

Once you've set your goals, you will need to monitor yourself to assess whether or not your goals are being met during practice. To monitor yourself effectively, you need to be focused and aware. Awareness requires that you totally focus your attention on a task, which is a skill you can develop as you practice your skating skills.

A good way to evaluate your focus is based on a technique called *focused hitting*. For figure skating, this technique can be adapted and used when skating a set pattern (such as a moves-in-the-field pattern), a figure, or a dance step. For example, choose a one-foot turn such as a three-turn, bracket, or counter that is relatively easy for you to do. Skate a figure-eight pattern, placing the turn at two specific spots on each circle, changing feet in the center of the figure eight. Perform this drill for three to five minutes. After the time is over, examine the print. Your markings on the ice illustrate the consistency in placement of the turn and are evidence of how focused you are.

This exercise is not only excellent for developing focus, but also for developing precision in your skating.

Another way to develop your awareness is through a procedure called *mindfulness*. This activity can be performed off-ice and involves sitting quietly, closing your eyes, and seeing how long you can focus on a single thought. Some athletes refer to this technique as "locking in" to their concentration zone. You can begin practicing locking in by practicing focusing while you are on the ice. Some skaters might lock in and focus on specific spots on the ice, or they might focus on what is necessary to execute the ideal movement. The key is to gently hold your attention on the predetermined task and, if your attention wanders, to gently bring it back to what you are doing. Perform this exercise on a regular basis if you know that you are easily distracted. It will help you to develop your mindfulness skills.

Awareness and Learning New Moves

Figure skating requires the mastery of many precise movement patterns. Learning new moves sometimes can be frustrating due to what sport psychologist Ken Ravizza refers to as the *all-or-none syndrome* (2001). When you are learning something new, you cannot expect complete mastery immediately. A series of progressions must be worked through. Sometimes in the process of developing an element, it seems like you're getting the feel for it. If you are, you feel great. But if you aren't, frustration begins to set in. The challenge is to keep yourself motivated throughout the hours of practice it takes to master the element.

To stay motivated, Ravizza suggests that you establish what those progressions are—what he calls *gradations of execution*—to evaluate your skill development fairly. For example, even if you don't land a jump, certain aspects of the jump were probably executed successfully, and it is important that you identify what those aspects were. You may have had a good flight position, but perhaps your landing foot position was not appropriate for a successful landing (e.g., the wrong part of the blade made first contact with the ice). To build awareness, it is essential that you reflect on the position of your skate. Your coach can then give you feedback based on how close you were to accurate performance. This evaluation can help you begin to adjust your awareness to what the proper position feels like. If a video camera is available, the performance feedback can be even more specific.

As you gain more awareness, you can begin to make more accurate adjustments in your performance. This ability to refine the subtleties of performance is a critical skill for reaching high-level performance. In addition to improving self-control, you also experience a feeling of growing success. Even though the outcome is not perfect, you develop a more positive attitude about the skill, which can help you to keep your motivation level where it needs to be when practicing.

Imagery

Having good imagery skills also can help you to develop awareness and focus, leading to more effective practice sessions. Imagery may be defined *as using all the senses to create or recreate an experience in your mind*. This definition of imagery includes three key points.

First, you can recreate, as well as create, experiences in your mind. You probably already use this technique quite often. During practice, have you ever watched another skater do a showy skating move and then turned around and done it yourself? Or maybe you've been able to improve your technique by watching the performance of a professional skater? You are able to imitate the actions of other people because you have a mental image of the skill that acts as a blueprint or guide for your performance, which is the fundamental principle behind imagery. Imagery is based on memory, and you experience it by reconstructing outside events in your mind. You can also create new experiences by combining familiar images in new ways. Whether you are creating or recreating a performance, imagery allows you to see it and believe it.

Second, you need to understand that imagery is not just about what you see. Imagery is sometimes called *visualization* or *seeing with the mind's eye*, but all the senses are important in experiencing events. When practicing imagery, strive toward creating images that involve all of the senses. In skating, doing so is particularly important because of the nature of the sport. You see the crowd and what's going on around you, but you must never look at your feet. You can hear the cut of your blades on the ice, the power of your music, and the support of the crowd. You can feel not only how you are holding your body in space, but also the sensations of the pressure of your boots, ice cuttings flying off your skates, and your blades pressing into the ice. You may associate many other scents and tastes with certain images as well. Being able to create images using all of your senses makes the images more real and believable.

The third point about imagery is that it happens without outside prompts. It occurs only in your mind. Research has shown that when athletes practice vivid imagery and become a part of that imagery, their brains interpret these images as if the actual performance was occurring. Using imagery in this way allows you to practice without being at the rink.

Imagery can be used in many ways in figure skating. You can use it to enhance how quickly you learn new skills. You can use it to prepare for competition. You can use it to calm yourself down or amp yourself up, whichever is needed. The first step is assessing what your current imagery skill level is. Then, once you've established your baseline, practice using imagery on a regular basis in a variety of different ways for a variety of different purposes. The Application Exercises in this chapter contain an assessment you can use to evaluate your imagery skills. You will learn a lot more about other uses of imagery in later chapters in this book.

Practice Routine

Having a predictable routine for practice sessions sets the stage for more productive practices. To get the most out of practices, include the following steps in your practice routine:

- Create a practice plan prior to arriving at the rink.
- Perform a mind-body warm-up prior to taking the ice.
- Practice mindfully, tuning in to what you are doing rather than tuning out or watching other skaters.
- Perform a mind-body cool-down after coming off the ice.

Jason R. Ross

You should perform a mind-body warm-up prior to taking the ice.

The Mind-Body Warm-Up

Always arrive at the rink in time to warm up your body and prepare your mind for practice. Your physical warm-up should include at least five minutes of dynamic, rhythmic movements (e.g., jumping rope, jogging, stepping up and down on a bench, running stairs), as well as static and dynamic stretching. See Poe (2002) for more information on what to include in a pre-practice, off-ice warm-up.

While performing your physical warm-up, start to prepare your mind for practice as well. As you are jumping rope, for example, check in with yourself to see what kind of mood you're in, and get yourself into a good, positive mindset if you're not already there (this subject will be discussed in more detail in the next chapter). As you stretch, think about your goals for the practice session or review them in your journal, and use imagery to practice perfectly before you step on the ice. As you put on your skates, think about the elements you are developing, and recreate them in your mind being performed with perfect technique. Plan to spend approximately 10 minutes performing this mind-body warm-up before stepping on the ice.

Practicing Mindfully

In your practice plan, you may have allotted yourself time limits to perform certain elements. During the time you are practicing a certain element, focus in on that element. Tune in to how it feels, where your body is in space, the sensations created by your blade and the boot. What "sound" does the element make? Examine the marking left by your move and use it to evaluate the quality of what you're doing.

This type of self-monitoring keeps you focused and more involved with your skating, which, in turn, makes your practice more productive. It also will allow you to more easily recall what works for you technique-wise and what does not.

The Mind-Body Cool-Down

After your practice session is over, perform a mind-body cool-down. For your mind, this exercise brings closure to the practice session. It also allows your body to cool down gradually, which is physiologically necessary for optimal development from a physical perspective. As you stretch, you also will relax your muscles and enhance your flexibility.

Plan to spend 10 to 15 minutes post-practice performing your cool-down. Take off your skates and find a warm environment in which to stretch. As you stretch, recall the day's practice. Consider what you did well during the session, as well as areas that require additional work. You may choose to write these ideas in your journal or just reflect on them. Closing your eyes and breathing deeply while stretching and reflecting will help you to relax as well.

In addition to reflecting, you also may choose to use this time to practice your imagery skills. For example, you might use this time to rehearse your pre-competition imagery program (more on this subject in Chapter 12). Or, you might perfectly practice elements in your mind that were challenging you on the ice during that day's practice. End your practice on a positive note, and leave the rink with a smile on your face, taking pleasure in the fact that each productive practice makes your skating stronger.

Research shows that, for advanced athletes who have practiced a sport for many years, differences in the level of expert performances are determined primarily by differences in the amount of focused, quality practice, and much less by differences in natural talent or inherited ability. So, to do your best in your sport, you need to be able to focus during practice and make a mental commitment to practicing with the highest possible quality. This chapter provides strategies.

Application Exercises

Exercise 1: Practice Planning

In your journal, design a weekly schedule (Figure 5-1). Write the sessions you skate and any other training you do in the schedule. Next, write a brief, general description on what you will practice in each session, as shown in the following example:

Monday 4 PM Freestyle (45 min)—Jumps and spins, program run-through
Tuesday 6 AM Freestyle (60 min)—Moves-in-the-field (MITF) patterns, power, dance steps

Monday	Tuesday	Wednesday	Thursday	Friday	Saturday	Sunday
4 PM FS	6 AM FS	6 AM FS	4 PM FS	6 AM FS	9 AM FS	
5 PM Strength training	Dance class	4 PM FS Off-ice jump	5 PM Strength training	4 PM FS	Lessons	

Figure 5-1. Sample weekly training schedule

Try to schedule at least 24 hours of recovery between heavy jump practice sessions. This recovery period assists with the critical muscular development and repair needed for preventing injuries caused by a high volume of jumping. It also helps skaters psychologically avoid boredom, frustration, and burnout that are often associated with excessive jump training.

Now, write goals for each practice session, including your off-ice sessions. Be sure to include a quality rating as well as the number of repetitions completed when it comes to technical skills. Don't forget to include goals around presentation skills and, as you start to learn them, psychological skills. From a mind-body conditioning perspective, these skills are best practiced as you are practicing your technical skills, and you may find some of the psychological skills to be useful during physical fitness training sessions as well.

Play around with advance practice planning and see what works for you. You might want to create at least an outline of your plans one or two weeks in advance. Or, you may prefer to take it day-by-day. Be flexible enough to modify your plans if your goals are not being met.

Exercise 2: Sport Imagery Evaluation (adapted from Vealey & Greenleaf, 2001)

As you complete this evaluation, remember that imagery is more than just visualizing something in your mind's eye. Vivid images may include the five senses: seeing, hearing, feeling, touching, and smelling. Vivid images may also include feeling emotions or moods. In this exercise, you will read descriptions of general sport situations. You are to imagine the situation and provide as much detail from your imagination as possible to make the image as real as you can. Then, rate your imagery in the following seven areas:

  a. How vividly you saw or visualized the image
  b. How clearly you heard the sounds
  c. How vividly you felt your body movements during the activity
  d. How clearly you were aware of your mood or felt your emotions of the situation
  e. Whether you could see the image from inside your body
  f. Whether you could see the image from outside your body
  g. How well you could control the image

After you read each description, think of a specific example of it—the skill, the people involved, the place, and the time. Then, close your eyes and take a few deep breaths to become as relaxed as you can. Put aside all other thoughts, and keep your eyes closed as you try to imagine the situation as vividly as possible. Of course, the scenarios you imagine are neither right nor wrong. Concentrate on using your imagery skills to create the most vivid and clear image that you can. After you have completed imagining each situation, rate your imagery skills in the previous seven areas using the following scales.

  • For items a through f, use the following scale:
    1 = No image present
    2 = Not clear or vivid, but a recognizable image
    3 = Moderately clear and vivid image

4 = Clear and vivid image

5 = Extremely clear and vivid image

- For item g, use the following scale:

  1 = No control at all of image

  2 = Very hard to control image

  3 = Moderate control of image

  4 = Good control of image

  5 = Complete control of image

Situation 1: Practicing Alone

Select one specific skill or activity in figure skating such as a sit spin. Now, imagine yourself performing this activity at the rink where you usually practice, without anyone else present. Close your eyes for about one minute, and try to see yourself at the rink—hear the sounds, feel your body perform the movement, and be aware of your state of mind or mood. Try to see yourself from behind your eyes or from inside your body. Then, try to see yourself from outside your body, as if you were watching yourself on television. Rate yourself on a scale of 1 to 5 on how well you:

a. Saw yourself doing the activity

b. Heard the sounds of doing the activity

c. Felt yourself making the movements

d. Were aware of your mood

e. Were able to see the image from inside your body

f. Were able to see the image from outside your body

g. Controlled the image

Situation 2: Practicing With Others

You are doing the same thing that you do when practicing alone, but now you are practicing the skill with your coach and other skaters present. This time, however, you make a mistake that everyone notices. Close your eyes for one minute to imagine yourself making the error and the type of situation it puts you in immediately afterward as vividly as you can. First, try to experience the feelings you have as you make the mistake. Then, quickly try to recreate the situation in your mind and imagine yourself correcting the mistake and performing perfectly. Try to see the image from behind your eyes or from inside your body as you correct the mistake. Next, try to see the image as if you were watching through a video camera. Rate yourself on a scale of 1 to 5 on how well you:

a. Saw yourself in this situation

b. Heard the sounds in this situation

c. Felt yourself making the movements

d. Felt the emotions of this situation

e. Were able to see the image from inside your body

f. Were able to see the image from outside your body

g. Controlled the image

Situation 3: Skating in Competition

Imagine yourself performing the same or similar activity in competition, but imagine yourself doing the activity very skillfully and the crowd showing appreciation for your efforts. As you imagine the situation, try to see the crowd and hear the noise they are making. Imagine yourself feeling confident in your ability to perform, as well as your ability to handle pressure. Now, close your eyes for about one minute and imagine this situation as vividly as possible. Try to imagine yourself performing from inside your body, as if you were actually performing, as well as from outside your body, as if you were a spectator. Rate yourself on a scale of 1 to 5 on how well you:

a. Saw yourself in this situation

b. Heard the sounds in this situation

c. Felt yourself making the movements

d. Felt the emotions of this situation

e. Were able to see the image from inside your body

f. Were able to see the image from outside your body

g. Controlled the image

Situation 4: Recalling a Peak Performance

Recall one of your all-time best performances—a performance in which you felt confident, in control, and in the zone. Close your eyes for about one minute and try to see yourself in that situation—feel your emotions and recreate the experience. Imagine your performance and recreate the feelings you experienced, both mentally and physically, during that performance. Try to see the image from within yourself, and then try to imagine the situation from outside yourself. Rate yourself on a scale of 1 to 5 on how well you:

a. Saw yourself in this situation

b. Heard the sounds in this situation

c. Felt yourself making the movements

d. Felt the emotions of this situation

e. Were able to see the image from inside your body

f. Were able to see the image from outside your body

g. Controlled the image

Scoring

Now, determine your imagery scores and see what they mean. Sum the ratings for each category and record them on the evaluation form (Figure 5-2). Interpret your scores in the visual, auditory, kinesthetic, emotion, and controllability categories based on the following scale:

Excellent: 18-20

Good: 15-17

Average: 12-14

Fair: 8-11

Poor: 4-7

	Dimension	Score
Sum all *a* items	Visual	
Sum all *b* items	Auditory	
Sum all *c* items	Kinesthetic	
Sum all *d* items	Emotion	
Sum all *e* items	Internal perspective	
Sum all *f* items	External perspective	
Sum all *g* items	Controllability	

Figure 5-2. Imagery skills evaluation

Notice the categories in which your scores were low. All of these categories are important for imagery training, so don't rely solely on your visual sense. Work to improve the other senses as well. Keep in mind that it takes practice, but you can increase your imagery ability.

Exercise 3: Establish a Practice Routine

Based on the guidelines provided in this chapter, briefly record your practice routine in your journal. Be sure to plan enough time for your warm-up and cool-down. Ideally, neither of these two activities will need to occur in the car on the way to the rink.

Positive Thinking and the Competitive Mindset

The concept of motivation and the important part it plays in becoming a better athlete was introduced in Chapter 1. Some of the techniques that you or your coach might use can be classified as positive or negative reinforcement. Positive techniques like praise and encouragement lead to greater and more rapid skill development, compared to negative techniques such as criticism. And positive techniques do not lead to the undesirable feelings of hurt, frustration, or resentment that often occur following negative reinforcement techniques.

Your thoughts happen so quickly both before and after doing something. How and what you think influences how you perform. Positive thinking can function as a positive reinforcement technique that you can use to improve both physical and psychological skill development. Your goal in this chapter is to learn how to cultivate positive thinking practices and use this type of thinking on a regular basis to achieve an effective competitive mindset.

The way you think when you practice and when you compete can mean the difference between a podium finish and a less successful result. Clearly, your thinking influences the quality of your skating. Leading coaches say that focused, quality practice—more so than talent and ability—makes the difference in elite skating performance.

The best skaters tell themselves things like, "I'm here to train, not to waste my time." In contrast, athletes who perform below their potential tell themselves things like, "It's not important—it's only practice." Adopting positive, productive thinking habits while practicing and competing leads to the development of an effective competitive mindset.

It makes sense, then, to focus on increasing or improving positive or productive thinking during practice and competition. At the same time, you should be aware of when your thoughts are negative or nonproductive. You need to know how to deal with those thoughts so you can continue to practice and perform to the best of your ability. Following are some strategies to keep you positive so you can get the most out of your practice sessions, performances, and competitions.

Strategies to Increase Positive Thinking During Practice

Like most everyone, you've probably had practices when you started off in a great mood, worked hard, gotten a lot out of the time, and just felt great about yourself afterward. Of course, you've probably also had those other kinds of practices when you are just going through the motions, falling on jumps you've landed in the past, or making so many mistakes that you get upset and your whole practice session is ruined.

The good news is that you are in control of how you think and feel. And it is possible to turn your thoughts and emotions around so they can work with you instead of against you. Following are a few strategies to improve your thinking so you can get the most out of your practices.

Strategy 1: Practice in a Positive Mood

As mentioned in the previous chapter, you get more out of practice if you're in the right mood. Before arriving at the rink, become aware of your mood. If you're in a good mood and looking forward to practicing, then go with those good, strong positive feelings. But if you're not in a good mood, you need to get there before you begin skating. Think about what you love about skating, what your strengths are, and what you have already accomplished in the sport. Or, you may think about other unrelated things that make you happy, like laughing with your best friend or remembering parts from a favorite movie. Use these memories, perhaps while putting on your skates or when warming up, to get yourself into a good mood before stepping on the ice. Once you've improved your mood, you're ready to start practicing.

Strategy 2: Have Specific Goals for Every Practice

The previous chapter also stressed the importance of creating a practice plan containing specific goals for the session. How can you reach your target if you don't know what you're aiming for? In skating, as in all pursuits, it's easier to feel like you're accomplishing something when you know what you're working toward.

The importance of goal setting has already been addressed. Part of being positive involves focusing on being productive. You're more productive when you prepare yourself for practice by setting some specific goals for that practice. Your goals might include working on a particular element until you have it performed to a certain level or grade of execution. You might instead choose goals that are related to the number of repetitions you'll attempt for each element. For example, you might choose to perform a particular jump combination on its own five times before skating it in your program. Or you might plan to practice your moves-in-the-field patterns in order three times as a warm-up prior to practicing your jumps and spins. Set a number of goals for yourself for each practice so that you're guaranteed to meet at least some of them.

Strategy 3: Focus on Your Progress

At some point, you will find yourself at a physical plateau with your skating. You won't seem to be able to master that one jump combination or footwork pattern, no matter how hard you practice. This situation can make practice frustrating—if you let it. But, rather than worrying about the element that's giving you trouble, think about the progress you've made over time.

One of the benefits of keeping a skating journal is that it can be a helpful tool for reminding yourself of your significant accomplishments during your skating journey. Compare yourself now to where you were at the beginning of the season or where you were last year at the same time. Are you performing new elements? Have you passed tests or placed higher in competition? Has the quality of specific elements improved? Are you skating faster and with more power? Are your presentation skills stronger? Answering questions like these will help you to focus on your progress rather than fixating on the element that is challenging you at the moment. When you look back at this point in time in the future, you'll appreciate even more the hard work you put into mastering that challenging skill.

Strategy 4: Use Energizing Self-Talk

The beginning of this chapter mentioned what elite skaters say to themselves compared to those messages that less-accomplished skaters tell themselves. What you say to yourself is called self-talk, and it's a tool you can use to keep your energy up and stay positive during practice. Rather than thinking about how tired you are or how heavy your legs might feel, which can zap your energy, think instead about words and phrases that will increase or sustain your energy, such as, "Use your edges," "You can do it," or "Really go for it."

Strategy 5: After Practice, Think About Something You Did Really Well

In the last chapter, the term *reflection* was mentioned as part of your mind-body cool-down following a practice session. To complete a successful practice, reflect on the session as a whole, and think about at least one or two things that you did quite well. If you keep a skating journal, make sure to record this information. If you prefer not to write things down, tell your coach or a fellow supportive skater what worked well for you and why you think so. The work and attention to detail you put into recording what led to your success will help you to recreate that experience at another practice or in competition. It may also help develop your imagery skills. Writing it down is like giving yourself a recipe for success.

Strategies for Decreasing Negative Thinking During Practice

Inevitably, you will have challenges during your practice sessions. You may experience things like difficulty mastering certain elements, distractions, bad program run-throughs, or numerous errors. You are human, and it's natural to feel upset when these kinds of things happen. However, if you're serious about your goals, you need to be able to turn these emotions around and get back to work. Learning how to turn negativity and upset feelings around makes you more productive and ensures that you don't ruin an entire session for yourself. If you find yourself getting upset, use the following strategies to turn your thinking around, and get back on track for a positive practice.

Strategy 1: Use Thought Stopping

When you hear the word *stop*, what images come to mind? Maybe it's a stop sign or a red light. Maybe it's your coach calling out to you. Whatever image reminds you to stop is the image you want to have in mind when you use this method. Thought stopping requires you to recognize when your thinking is negative or nonproductive. Although you may not be aware of negative thinking until you're already quite upset, the best use of thought stopping is early detection of the negative thought or emotion, followed by a vivid, purposeful image of your stop signal. Once you've had your negative thought, you need to replace it with something more positive and useful. Choose from the remaining strategies to help you get back into a positive mindset.

Strategy 2: Skate a "Positive Thinking" Lap

When you're upset, it's hard to focus on what you're working on. You're likely to repeat the same mistakes and not make any progress when you're in that frame of mind. When you find yourself "losing it," give yourself permission to stop what you're doing and skate a purposeful "positive thinking" lap. As you're skating your lap, use positive self-talk to put things into perspective and adopt a more focused attitude. Remember that getting upset is natural, but knowing how to stay positive will help you make better use of your practice time. This ability adds up to smarter and more productive practice.

Strategy 3: Model a Hardworking, Cheerful Skater

Chances are, you're not the only one practicing during a session. If you find yourself getting upset, skate to the side of the rink, look around, and find another skater who is focused and working hard. Watch this skater for a few moments, and notice the things that tell you that the skater is in tune with what she is practicing. Then, try to replicate those things and model this hardworking skater. Be sure to do this exercise discreetly—do not distract the skater you're modeling. Tell yourself, "If she can do it, so can I."

Strategy 4: Remind Yourself Why You Love to Skate

Reminding yourself why you love to skate was introduced as a way to put yourself in a positive mood. This strategy is also a good thing to do when you're finding yourself getting frustrated or upset. Skate to the side of the rink, take a few calming breaths, and remind yourself of the pleasure and enjoyment you derive from skating. Don't let a less-than-perfect aspect of your practice take this joy away from you. Instead, think about how good it will feel when you've mastered the challenge you're currently facing.

Strategy 5: Be Your Own Best Friend

Think about your best friend. When she is down, what do you say to help? You probably encourage your best friend with cheerful and kind words to make her feel better. You should try to be your own best friend, especially in times of difficulty during practice. Rather than saying things to yourself like, "I'm never going to land this jump" or "This move is taking too long to learn," think about what your best friend would say to cheer you up. You can use this type of self-talk to encourage yourself to turn things around and stay positive.

Strategy 6: Defuse Overreactions

When you think negative, nonproductive thoughts like, "I'm never going to land this jump," you are simply overreacting to a current limitation of physical skill proficiency. Such thoughts are self-defeating and untrue. They also can interfere with your progress and take the fun out of skating. In these instances, you need to use thought stopping, and logic needs to take over. You are getting upset because you want to master the element, but it's likely that you haven't set reasonable expectations to evaluate your progress. Effective goal setting and keeping a skating journal can help in this instance. Even if you keep a weekly skating journal as opposed to a daily one, you should be able to see your progress in the various aspects of your skating. It's important to stay focused on a goal of progression rather than complete mastery, so you can keep yourself from getting frustrated with the learning process.

Using Positive Self-Talk During Competition

Whether you know it or not, you're thinking about something when you skate your programs. Just like you practice your physical elements, you must also practice positive self-talk or positive thinking so that you automatically will be positive when you compete. It makes no sense to spend so much time on footwork, jumps, and spins, and then leave your mindset to chance. If you don't plan and practice positive thoughts as you practice your physical skills, you stand a greater chance that negative or distracting thoughts will enter your mind during a competition.

You've learned about using self-talk during practice to get and stay energized and to turn around negative thinking. Having well-planned self-talk and key words will help you to stay focused and think about what you're doing during each element of your program, and it will prevent you from thinking ahead to more difficult jumps or moves. It will even help with recovery after a fall or an error in your program. Maybe you've previously let one missed element spoil the rest of your program. You continued to think about that mistake, beating yourself up over it. This behavior only makes you more nervous and upset, which interferes with your focus for the remaining elements.

You need to recognize that you can't change the past. When you've attempted an element on a particular run-through, it's gone. You can't get it back. So why worry about it? Why not go on to the next element? Again, having well-planned self-talk and key words will help you do just that.

During the stress of competition, when you may be feeling more pressure or experiencing more distractions, well-practiced self-talk and key words will take over and help you to perform well. When you focus on the self-talk that you've used many times during run-throughs at practice, the elements are more likely to be there during a competition.

Athletes perform best when they are completely in control of their performances. Well-practiced self-talk and key words help athletes stay focused and in the moment. A former world pairs champion remarked that to stay completely in the moment, he had to think about every arm movement, every gesture, and every move of the skate— something that took him four years to learn how to do consistently during his programs.

Exercise 2 in the Application Exercises at the end of this chapter guides you through the process of creating effective self-talk and key words for your programs. Once you've established your self-talk and key words, it's important to practice them each time you run through your programs. Practice your program self-talk and key words as you skate your program in practice, as well as when you walk through your program off-ice. The more you practice, the easier it will be for the words to automatically come to mind during competition.

Remember that increasing positive thinking and defusing negative thoughts takes practice. Using your key words and positive self-talk during practice will not only help you hone these skills, but this discipline will also keep you more focused—and that only increases the chances of a more productive session.

Program: Juvenile free skate		
Element	Coach's Reminders	Additional Prompts
Lutz	Stay on the outside edge	Breathe, take your time
Falling leaf	None	Open
Back sit spin	Back straight but bent at a 60-degree angle to leg; finish "fast"	Exhale and extend
Axel	Punch through the arms; strong exit	Tight
Footwork	Strong and controlled; powerful, deep edges	Energy
Flip	None	Lift
Camel-change-camel	Straighten skating leg; right arm pulls toward left free foot on back camel	Smooth, controlled
Loop-toe-loop combination	Place the toe	Up and up
Layback spin	Extend the spine, then round over; pretty hands	Centered

Figure 6-1. Sample self-talk for program elements

Application Exercises

Exercise 1: Apply the Strategies

Choose at least two of the strategies from this chapter to implement during practice. Note in your skating journal which strategies you chose and why. Log your progress in terms of how often and at what quality/ability the strategies were used during your practice sessions. After a day, a week, or three weeks, evaluate how well you were able to use the strategies and how using the strategies has helped your skating.

Exercise 2: Plan and Practice Self-Talk for Competition

To teach yourself how to stay in the moment and in better control of your competitive performance, create a table in your skating journal like the one in Figure 6-1. Use it to plan realistic and helpful self-talk to use when skating your programs. List the elements you have in your current program in the first column (make separate tables for each program you skate). Next, for difficult elements, think about the reminders your coach has given you for setting them up (e.g., shoulders square, right side together, stretch up, etc.). In the center column, write the reminders of what you should focus on when setting up each element. In the final column, add any additional prompts to help you stay relaxed and in control, to focus on one element at a time, and to sell your program and present it well. Prompts that skaters have used include things like, "Go for it," "Work the edges," "Graceful," "Deep knee bend," and so on. Keep them short so that they are easy to remember. Practice this planned self-talk when you practice your program run-throughs on the ice and when you practice program walk-throughs off the ice.

7

Social Physique Anxiety and Other Body-Image Issues

The previous chapter discussed self-talk as a method you can use to create a positive mindset. As you become more aware of your own self-talk, you may begin to realize that you sometimes use self-talk in a way that is harmful to you. This chapter introduces specific psychological challenges involved with participating in an *aesthetic* sport—a sport that favors a specific look or body type. It addresses *social physique anxiety*, a condition that involves negative self-talk and its impact on aesthetic athletes like figure skaters.

When social physique anxiety is not addressed, it may develop into full-blown body-image disturbances and eating disorders. You'll learn about these conditions and what you can do instead to develop a healthy, more aesthetically pleasing physique. This chapter concludes with a body image mapping exercise and a proactive application exercise designed to help you discover healthy methods for improving the appearance of your physique.

Social Physique Anxiety

Social physique anxiety and body image are psychological constructs that describe how you feel about your body. While they aren't exactly the same thing, they are related and may predict how likely you are both to perform well in sports and to engage in other physical activities.

Social physique anxiety is the anxiety you experience when you think other people are evaluating your physique negatively. If you experience higher levels of social physique anxiety, you might think, for example, that other people think you're too thin, or too heavy, or too fat, and so on. Females are much more likely to suffer from social physique anxiety than men, and female athletes who participate in aesthetic sports are much more likely to experience some degree of social physique anxiety, especially as they approach puberty and mature sexually. Social physique anxiety can become a performance issue if its effects impact your ability to skate well in front of an audience or a judging panel.

While social physique anxiety and body image aren't exactly the same thing, they are related and may predict how likely you are both to perform well in sports and to engage in other physical activities.

Body Image

Psychologists define body image as *a multidimensional construct that reflects how you see your own body and how you think, feel, and act toward it*. The four dimensions of body image are perceptual, cognitive, affective or emotional, and behavioral.

The *perceptual* dimension of body image reflects the picture of your body that you form in your mind (i.e., how you see yourself when you look in the mirror and how you imagine yourself to look). The way you imagine yourself to look may or may not be the same as how you actually look.

The *cognitive* dimension of body image reflects how you think about or evaluate your body in terms of both its appearance and function. For example, you may choose to view your muscular legs as being *huge* or as being *powerful*, depending on whether you're evaluating how you think they look compared to how you think they function.

The *affective* or *emotional* dimension of body image reflects the feelings you experience in relation to your body's appearance and function. For example, if you choose to think about your muscular legs as being huge, you may feel badly about yourself in general, and your legs in particular, especially when your legs are on display in a short skating dress and tights.

The *behavioral* dimension of body image represents the things you do that reflect your positive or negative perceptions—your thoughts and feelings—about your body, such as the type of clothing you wear and the activities you choose to engage in. People are said to have healthy body images if they give themselves positive evaluations across the four dimensions. However, if people report negative self-evaluations along any or all of the body-image dimensions, they are said to have a *body image disturbance*.

Why does body image disturbance occur? It has to do with comparing your body *reality* with a body *ideal*. This body ideal might be created by media influences, cultural influences, activity participation (desiring a specific body type based on the activity you perform), and changes to your body reality (e.g., maturing/going through puberty).

Body image is important because it affects both your physical and your psychological well-being. Having a body image disturbance can lead to health-damaging behaviors such as developing eating disorders, engaging in unhealthy weight-control strategies, and smoking. Psychologically, body image disturbance is also associated with low self-esteem, depression, and anxiety.

Eating Disorders

When a body image disturbance becomes serious enough, it may lead to a clinically diagnosed eating disorder. Eating disorders this severe are not that common among athletes, but they do tend to occur more frequently in aesthetic sports such as figure skating, gymnastics, and diving. In fact, one of the best known examples of a sports-related eating disorder is that of Christy Henrich, a former U.S. Olympic gymnast. At the young age of 22, Christy died from anorexia nervosa, an eating disorder she suffered from for over eight years.

Anorexia nervosa is one of the two most severe types of eating disorders. Bulimia nervosa is the other. Clinical psychologists usually make these diagnoses following specific criteria. Only a small percentage of girls and women in North America suffer from these serious eating disorders, but subclinical levels of eating disorders seem to be more common, especially among athletes.

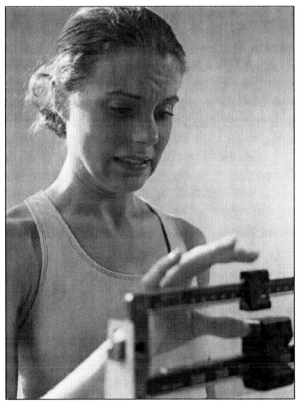

When a body image disturbance becomes serious enough, it may lead to a clinically diagnosed eating disorder.

Anorexia Nervosa

People diagnosed with anorexia nervosa are often referred to as anorexics. Anorexics do not eat very much. Instead, they move their food around their plates, take tiny bites of food, and chew each bite excessively. They become obsessed with rigid control over their food intake, weight, and size. They often will dress in loose, layered clothing to hide their thinness. To burn fat and calories, anorexics often exercise excessively. Treatment and recovery from anorexia nervosa requires professional help. Diagnosed anorexics cannot overcome this condition on their own. The criteria for an anorexia nervosa diagnosis include:

- Severe weight loss
- Refusal to maintain normal body weight
- Intense fear of gaining weight or becoming fat
- Severe body image disturbance
- Absence of three or more consecutive menstrual cycles

Bulimia Nervosa

People diagnosed with bulimia nervosa are called bulimics. Bulimics are preoccupied with food, their weight, and their amount of body fat. Bulimics exhibit chaotic eating patterns referred to as bingeing and purging. During an eating binge, a bulimic eats excessively and compulsively. Purging, or getting rid of the excessive food intake, may include self-induced vomiting, using laxatives, diuretics, or enemas, or a combination of these tactics. Eating binges also may be followed by periods of fasting, excessive exercise, or vomiting. Several physical signs and symptoms are associated with frequent vomiting, including finger calluses, sore throat, bloating, stomach alkalosis, and chemical imbalance. As with anorexia nervosa, treatment and recovery from bulimia nervosa requires professional help. The criteria for a bulimia nervosa diagnosis include:

- Binge eating followed by purging at least twice per week for three months
- Loss of self-control
- Severe body image disturbance

Subclinical Eating Disorders Among Athletes

Subclinical eating disorders (i.e., disorders that do not fulfill clinical diagnosis criteria) are the greatest concern for many female athletes participating in sports that encourage low body weight and thinness. Subclinical eating disorders are far more prevalent among female athletes than anorexia nervosa or bulimia nervosa.

Males and females involved in sports that link leanness to success are often pressured to be thin. This concept is especially true of female athletes involved in gymnastics, dance, and figure skating. In an effort to be thin and to meet their coaches' expectations, skaters may try questionable eating and exercise behaviors that can cause them harm. In most cases, the desire to be thin does not result in clinically diagnosed anorexia or bulimia. At some point though, if left unchecked, subclinical eating disorders may result in dysfunctional social interaction, decreased physical performance, reduced physical health, and, in some cases, anorexia or bulimia. People with subclinical eating disorders may use the following methods to control their weight. The consequences of using these unhealthy methods of weight control are listed in Figure 7-1.

- Fasting/starvation
- Diet pills
- Diuretics
- Laxatives/enemas
- Vomiting
- Fat-free diets
- Saunas
- Excessive exercise

When it comes to subclinical eating disorders, research has found that:
- Athletes report more eating disorder symptoms than nonathletes.
- Athletes who compete in aesthetic sports (e.g., gymnastics, dance, diving, figure skating) report more eating disorders than those who compete in nonaesthetic sports.
- Athletes in general, do not have a greater drive for thinness than nonathletes.

At some point, if left unchecked, subclinical eating disorders may result in dysfunctional social interaction, decreased physical performance, reduced physical health, and, in some cases, anorexia or bulimia.

Behavior	Health Consequences
Diet pills	Heightened anxiety, rapid heart rate, poor concentration, insomnia, dehydration
Diuretics	Dehydration, electrolyte imbalance, little fat loss, weight loss quickly regained
Excessive exercise	Menstrual dysfunction in females, fatigue, increased risk of overuse injuries, hunger following exercise
Fasting/starvation	Loss of lean body mass and bone density, poor physical and cognitive performance, lack in essential nutrients
Fat-free diets	Difficulty in maintaining weight loss, possible lack in essential vitamins, nutrients, and fatty acids
Laxatives/enemas	Dehydration, electrolyte imbalance, constipation, cathartic colon
Saunas	Dehydration, electrolyte imbalance, no permanent weight loss
Self-induced vomiting	Dehydration, electrolyte imbalance, gastrointestinal problems, stomach ulcers, erosion of tooth enamel

Figure 7-1. Unhealthy weight control behaviors and their negative consequences

One final area of recent interest related to subclinical eating disorders is the phenomenon known as the *female athlete triad*. The American College of Sports Medicine has published a position paper on this topic, and presentations addressing the female athlete triad have been made at some of the most recent seminars on sports science and medicine relating to figure skating. The female athlete triad refers to three distinct conditions that tend to occur together in female athletes: eating disorders, amenorrhea, and osteoporosis.

Amenorrhea refers to abnormalities of menstrual cycles. Most females start their menses by age 16 and typically have 10 to 13 periods each year. It is normal for some irregularity to occur when a female first starts her period, but it is *not* normal to lose menses completely. Any change or abnormality in a female's menstrual cycle should be evaluated.

Osteoporosis is the formal name for thin bones. Bone density is usually achieved between the ages of 20 and 30, and slowly decreases with age. Adolescence is a time when bone mass should be built up, but abnormal menses decreases estrogen levels, which in turn can cause early bone loss, eventually resulting in osteoporosis. Thin bones increase the risk of stress fractures and other types of fractures.

Eating Disorder Symptoms in Figure Skaters

One study (Taylor & Ste-Marie, 2001) showed that female pair skaters and dance figure skaters were more similar to an eating-disordered population than to a comparison sample of college-aged females. In the study, 92.7 percent of the skaters responded "yes" to the question, "Do you think there are pressures associated with figure skating to lose weight or maintain a below-average weight?" All of the figure skaters had engaged in weight-control methods at some point in their skating careers, using the following methods:

- Fasting, dieting, and/or excessive exercise (78%)
- Vomiting and/or diet pills (39%)
- All of the unhealthy weight-control methods associated with subclinical eating disorders (23%)

© Bela Szandelszky/Red Dot/ZUMA Press

One research study that was conducted showed that female pair skaters and dance figure skaters were more similar to an eating-disordered population than to a comparison sample of college-aged females.

Building a Healthy Physique

It would be misleading to suggest that the aesthetic aspect of figure skating does not favor a lean body type. However, leanness and thinness are two different things. Being lean does not necessarily mean being at a low or unhealthy weight. Athletes can build a lean, healthy physique that not only will look more attractive, but also will facilitate their sport performance. Achieving this type of physique is accomplished through exercise, nutrition, and other healthful practices based on exercise science.

Exercise—Good for the Body and the Mind

In addition to all of the physical benefits that regular exercise provides, exercise has also been shown to have significant psychological effects, including improved mood, decreased anxiety, and increased feelings of relaxation, calmness , and satisfaction. Both aerobic and resistance training have demonstrated these positive effects on psychological health and emotional well-being. So participating in a regular conditioning program outside of your practice time on the ice will not only improve your fitness level and sport performance, but it may also help you feel happier and healthier more of the time.

Exercise has also been shown to lead to significant improvements in body image. Some studies have even found that exercise is just as effective as psychological interventions for improving body image. Of course, unlike psychological interventions, exercise has the added bonus of improving your health and physical fitness at the same time.

Several possibilities could explain why exercise makes you feel better about your body. One idea is that you feel better about your body because of the improved physical fitness. The research, so far, is mixed in terms of whether it's *actual* or *perceived* changes in physical fitness that trigger improvements in body image. It may be that the changes in body image are attributable to actual improvements in fitness or perceived improvements in physical appearance. In other words, is it the actual changes in strength and endurance that make you feel better about your body? Or is it the changes in physical appearance that accompany improved fitness that make you feel better about your body?

Another idea is that when you exercise, you become more aware of your physical capabilities. For example, you might not be able to achieve the "ideal" figure skating physique through exercise alone, but it is possible to improve your physical functioning and conditioning through exercise. Research shows that when females exercise to improve nonappearance aspects of body image (such as satisfaction with physical function), they are more likely to experience success and satisfaction than when they exercise for appearance-related reasons.

A third idea is that exercise improves body image because it increases your belief in yourself and your physical capabilities—what is known as your *physical self-efficacy*. When you work with a fitness professional who is trained to develop effective exercise programs for figure skaters, that person will design a program for you that will demonstrate your physical capabilities and monitor your improvement in a very objective manner. As your physical capabilities improve, it is likely than your physical self-efficacy also improves. Such changes in self-efficacy may be what lead to changes in body image.

In addition to your on-ice training, consider participating in a more comprehensive fitness program designed by a qualified strength and conditioning or fitness professional. More information on how to locate a qualified professional is included in the Application Exercises.

Nutrition—You Are What You Eat

Nutrition is vitally important for all athletes. The food and drinks that you consume provide the energy that fuels your body. When you fuel your body well, you feel good, strong, and capable of skating for hours. When you do not fuel your body well, you don't feel good, and you may even feel weaker as a result.

In addition to affecting how you feel and your ability to practice, perform, and compete, what and how you eat also impacts your body composition. Body composition was introduced in the pre-season assessment, and it's an important measurement that differs from weight in a significant way. Body composition compares how much of your body's weight is composed of lean mass (e.g., bones, muscles, organs) with how much of your body's weight is composed of adipose tissue or fat mass. Muscle weighs more than fat, but it takes up much less space under the surface of your skin. You can appear very lean and compact but weigh more than someone who appears larger in size simply due to having more of your weight made up of lean mass relative to fat mass.

If part of your training includes improving your body's aesthetic appearance, your goal should be decreasing fat mass and increasing lean mass rather than focusing on weight loss. A certified strength and conditioning or fitness professional should be able to assess and monitor your body composition effectively and design a program that trains for this specific result. A registered dietitian should be consulted to determine the best nutritional plan to meet the demands of this goal and your other goals associated with figure skating.

Use these kinds of professionals instead of taking unhealthy steps to attempt to modify your body composition on your own. Trained professionals are well-versed in the exercise sciences that produce the results you're after, without producing the adverse affects that the less healthy weight-control methods produce. When left to their own devices, the weight loss that most people experience is a combination of decreases in both lean mass and fat mass. Losing lean mass is generally *not* desirable for any athlete, as it is associated with decreases and limitations in muscular strength and endurance as well as in performance.

In addition to the food you are eating, it is equally important to pay attention to what you are drinking. Another healthy practice associated with building a healthy physique is staying hydrated. The effects of dehydration on athletic performance are getting more research attention, and how to stay hydrated when you are physically active for extended periods of time is a topic you should discuss with your nutrition professional as part of your nutrition plan. Active bodies need much more hydration than you may think—likely more often than just when you *feel* thirsty. By the time you feel thirsty, chances are, you're already dehydrated. Dehydration has been shown to produce decreased performance, which means it can impact your ability to practice, train, perform, and compete. Often, rapid weight loss is a result of dehydration, demonstrating again why unhealthy weight-control practices can lead to impairments in performance. Your nutrition professional can make specific recommendations regarding how frequently and what types of drinks you should be consuming to keep yourself hydrated and healthy.

Rest, Recovery, and Sleep

The importance of rest and recovery can not be overestimated. Exercise science has shown that improvements in motor learning, muscle memory, and muscle development happen more readily when appropriate rest and recovery are implemented. The concept of periodization was introduced in a previous chapter. Periodization refers to training differently depending on where you are in your competitive season. A periodized athletic training program includes not only the training you do on the ice and the conditioning you perform off-ice, but also recovery time between workouts. Training *more* is not the same thing as training *smart*, and performance can be impacted if you overtrain, meaning you are not allowing for enough rest and recovery between your training sessions.

In addition to resting between workouts, having healthy sleeping habits is also important to produce a healthy physique. Strive to consistently sleep at least eight hours most nights of the week, and take naps as often as your body feels it necessary. When you push your body hard, one of its natural recovery responses is to go to sleep. During sleep is the time when important repair work occurs in your body. When your sleep patterns are interrupted, research has shown that your body's ability to heal itself is also disrupted.

Feeling good or feeling bad about your body is within your control, and it's something that impacts your ability to perform at your best. Understanding social physique anxiety and body image disturbance can help you understand if you may be engaging in self-talk that is more harmful than helpful. If you do have concerns about the appearance of your physique, seek the advice of certified health and fitness professionals, and learn the healthy habits associated with creating a strong, healthy athletic physique.

Application Exercises

Exercise 1: Creating a Body Image Map

To gain insight into your body image, consider creating a body image map. Using a large sheet of butcher paper, draw an outline of your body, trying to make the drawing as accurate as possible in terms of height, width, shape, and so forth. Once you've created your outline, take a look at it, and think about how you feel about the following parts of your body:

• Shoulders	• Upper arms	• Buttocks
• Chest	• Lower arms	• Upper legs
• Stomach	• Hips	• Lower legs

Mark on your diagram how you feel about each of those body parts, using the following symbols. Do you see a connection among the symbols on your diagram, the body parts you work out the most during skating and other forms of exercise, and the types of clothes you like to wear?

- Stars = body parts you like to show off
- Smiley faces = body parts you're content with
- Neutral faces = body parts that you feel neutral about
- Frown faces = body parts you want to hide

Now, lie down on your drawing and either trace or have a friend trace the actual outline of your body. Are there differences between how you drew your body and how it is actually shaped? What do you think this difference says about your body image?

Exercise 2: Build Your Health While Building Your Physique

If you are not already working with health and fitness professionals, now is the perfect time to start exploring this possibility. Even if your goal is not to change the appearance of your physique, implementing an appropriate conditioning program will improve your health as well as your athletic performance. To find certified professionals who specialize in conditioning for figure skaters, consult resources provided by U.S. Figure Skating, the American College of Sports Medicine, the American Council on Exercise, or the National Strength and Conditioning Association. The American Dietetic Association can provide resources to qualified registered dietitians. Take advantage of opportunities to meet these professionals at seminars and competitive events.

Relaxation and Arousal Deactivation Techniques

In this chapter and the next, you will start to examine energy or arousal levels and determine how energized you need to be to perform at your best, both at practice and in competition. Some sport psychologists refer to a "performance thermometer," in which athletes evaluate their energy or arousal levels like they would gauge temperature. For example, some athletes need to be really psyched up or "hot" to perform at their best. Others need to be calm and "cool." And still others need to be somewhere in between. Think about your own performance thermometer and where you are when you perform at your best.

Once you understand where you perform at your best, the next step is to learn how to regulate your ability to achieve your optimal energy levels at will. Sometimes you'll need to increase your energy or arousal levels, and other times, you might need to relax and decrease those levels. In this chapter, you'll learn how to calm yourself down by learning relaxation or arousal deactivation techniques.

Practicing relaxation techniques helps you decrease your stress levels and increase self-awareness. In addition to helping you perform better, learning to relax helps you communicate more effectively, set clearer goals and values, evaluate problems more constructively, and dream up more creative solutions. Relaxation is essential for maintaining optimal health and well-being and for preventing stress-related illnesses.

Both your body and your mind behave differently when you're relaxed compared to when you are feeling stressed. The relaxation response is the opposite of the stress response and is governed by the activation of the parasympathetic nervous system, one branch of your nervous system. This division of the autonomic nervous system is primarily responsible for conserving and restoring energy during times of rest and recovery. When this system is active, several things happen: heart rate slows, the force of the heart's contraction decreases, blood pressure returns to a resting level, breathing becomes slower and deeper, skeletal muscles relax, the production of stress hormones stops, and your body recovers its homeostasis or balance.

Relaxation techniques are used for treating many stress-related disorders including headaches, gastrointestinal problems, insomnia, high blood pressure, anxiety, and heart disease. These techniques are also becoming popular for easing the pain of childbirth, treating addiction, and helping people cope with chronic pain. They have been used successfully with all kinds of subjects, including healthy people, hospital patients, children, adolescents, and college students. These techniques are especially helpful for people who are "hot reactors" (i.e., those who startle or feel stressed easily and tend to overreact physically to stress, as well as those with stress-related illnesses). Almost everyone can benefit from learning something about relaxation, even if it is just a few simple breathing exercises to help you fall asleep more easily during times of stress.

Jason R. Ross

Almost everyone can benefit from learning something about relaxation, even if it is just a few simple breathing exercises to help you fall asleep more easily during times of stress.

At the end of your practice session, slowly bring your focus back to the here and now, gently stretch your muscles, and open your eyes if they were closed.

Guidelines for Practice

Following are some guidelines that apply to all of the relaxation techniques you'll learn in this chapter:

- Schedule a convenient time and place to practice, and do so regularly. People often utilize these techniques as a last resort rather than being proactive. If you cannot control your thoughts and feelings during stress-free times, it will be almost impossible to do during high-stress times.
- Get as comfortable as possible. Loosen tight clothing, sit or lie comfortably, and use props such as pillows and blankets if you like.
- Try *not* to try. Keep a passive attitude and observe without judging what is occurring. The harder you try, the tenser you will get. Let go of judgment and expectation, let go of extraneous thoughts.
- Avoid falling asleep. Relaxation requires concentration and active awareness—it's not the same as lethargy. If your goal is not to fall asleep, open your eyes, practice in a well-lit room, and use a seated position.
- Finish relaxation sessions by coming back slowly. At the end of your practice session, slowly bring your focus back to the here and now, gently stretch your muscles, and open your eyes if they were closed.

Some people experience increased anxiety when they practice relaxation—a discomfort with "letting go" and a fear that they are losing control. If you are one of those people, choose techniques you feel most comfortable with, and build up your practice slowly.

Relaxation Techniques

In sport psychology, relaxation techniques are often divided into two categories: Muscle-to-mind techniques and mind-to-muscle techniques. This distinction is made depending on the starting point—the body or the mind—of the relaxation technique.

Muscle-to-mind techniques are based on the idea that you can tune into sensations or feelings in your physical body and learn how to allow the musculature and body systems to relax or slow down, resulting in a more calm mind as well. Some examples that you'll learn about in this chapter include the body scan, breathing exercises, progressive relaxation, and hatha yoga.

Mind-to-muscle techniques work the opposite way. The initial focus is on calming the mind, and as a result, your body's musculature and systems also relax or slow down. Some examples that you'll learn about in this chapter include meditation, visualization, autogenic training (a form of self-hypnosis), and positive affirmations.

Some techniques may resonate with you more than others. Figure skaters and other people who are very kinesthetically aware seem to respond to the muscle-to-mind techniques, whereas cerebral people often prefer mind-to-muscle. By learning about and practicing a variety of methods, you're sure to discover which techniques work best for you.

Muscle-to-Mind Techniques

The Body Scan

The body scan is a good way to begin any relaxation session. Begin by sitting or lying in a comfortable position—eyes may be open or closed. Turn your attention to the sensations in your body. Begin at your toes and note any sensations such as tension, relaxation, pain, warmth, coolness, heaviness, floating, or no sensation. Work your way up your body, beginning with one leg, and then the other. Scan the ankles, calves, shins, knees, thighs, and buttocks. Compare your legs. Does one side feel tighter? Heavier? Warmer? Note any differences. Do the same for your arms, starting first on one side with the fingers, hand, wrist, forearm, elbow, and upper arm, then scan the other and compare sides.

Continue scanning your pelvis, abdomen, chest, lower back, upper back, shoulders, and neck. Gently roll your head from side to side. Notice where your neck feels loose and where any tightness occurs. Now, become aware of your facial muscles, including the muscles of your forehead, the area between your eyebrows, the muscles around your eyes, your jaw, and tongue. Tune in to the muscles of your scalp.

Now, repeat your scan. Have any sensations changed? Do any areas feel more relaxed? Less relaxed? Make a mental note of the areas where you feel tension. Common areas of tension include the legs, hands, pelvis, abdomen, chest, back, shoulders, neck, and face. Take a big stretch, and open your eyes if they were closed.

A variation of this exercise is to perform the scan with suggestions to each body part to relax. After scanning your body with awareness, repeat the scan while imagining that each part is letting go and becoming more relaxed.

Breathing Exercises

Deep breathing is the easiest and most accessible relaxation technique. It can be used any time and any place and has often been called the bridge between the body and the mind. It can occur as an automatic or a conscious act. Most of the time, you probably give little thought to your breathing. The next time you get stressed, notice what happens to your breathing. It tends to become shallow and irregular, and your chest may feel constricted. It is natural to hold your breath when you're stressed.

Breathing Awareness

Perform this technique while lying down. Breathe exclusively through the nose if possible. Become aware of your breathing and the movement that occurs as you inhale and exhale. Place your hand where you feel the most movement—the place that seems to rise and fall the most as you breathe. If this spot is in your chest, your breathing could be more relaxed.

Now, bring the breath deeper into your belly. Place both hands over your navel. Feel your belly rise and fall with each breath. This place is where the most movement will occur when you are relaxed. Now, keep one hand on your belly and place the other on your chest. Can you feel your chest moving in harmony with your abdomen, or is it tight and rigid? Try *not* to try, but relax and allow this breathing to develop naturally. Finish by scanning your body for tension. Pay special attention to your belly, chest, throat, jaw, and other facial muscles.

Alternate Nostril Breathing

Perform this exercise seated with good posture. You may choose to close your eyes. Rest your index and middle finger of your right hand on your forehead. Close your right nostril with your thumb. Inhale slowly through your left nostril. Now, close your left nostril with your ring finger and open your right nostril. Exhale through your right nostril. Inhale through your right nostril. Close your right nostril with your thumb and open your left nostril. Exhale through the left nostril. Continue the cycle. Once you get used to this technique, try to make your exhalations twice as long as your inhalations.

Deep Breathing

This exercise may be performed either seated or lying down. It is often referred to as the three-part breath and becomes smoother with practice as each of the three parts only takes a few seconds.

Place one hand on your abdomen and the other on your chest, as you did during the breathing awareness exercise. As you inhale, feel your belly rise. After filling the lower portion of your lungs with air, keep inhaling, filling the middle portion of your lungs in your lower chest. You will feel the hand on your chest rise and your ribs expand. Continue to inhale and feel the air filling your upper lungs. You will feel your collarbone rise as your lungs fill completely.

Exhale slowly, from the top of your lungs to the bottom. Near the end of your exhalation, allow your abdominal muscles to contract slightly, pushing out the last bit of air. The exhalation phase of the breath is when relaxation occurs. To increase relaxation, lengthen the exhalation. Once deep breathing feels natural, let the exhalation phase become twice as long as your inhalation. You may also include short pauses between the inhalations and exhalations.

You can add mental imagery to your deep breathing. Place one hand on your solar plexus (the area just above your waist and navel). As you inhale, imagine energy gathering in your solar plexus. You might visualize this energy as a ball of light, growing larger and brighter as you inhale. As you exhale, imagine this energy flowing out to all parts of your body. If one part of your body is injured or in pain, place one hand there, and send the light to that part as you exhale.

Progressive Relaxation

Progressive relaxation is a muscle-to-mind technique that involves tensing and relaxing your muscles in a sequential order. For example, you might begin by tensing your right hand for five to seven seconds, and then actively releasing the tension and relaxing for 20 to 30 seconds. You work your way up your right arm, and then over to the left arm, and then both arms together. As you learn to release more and more, you learn to really *feel* the difference between when your muscles are tense and when they are relaxed. A guided progressive relaxation practice is included in the Application Exercises at the end of this chapter.

Hatha Yoga

Hatha yoga is a form of physical activity that induces relaxation. *Yoga* is a Sanskrit word that roughly translates as "yoke" or "union," and this activity often is described as a union of the body, mind, and spirit. The practice of yoga is said to consist of eight limbs or branches. Hatha yoga is the branch of yoga that emphasizes physical postures that incorporate breath control and mental concentration. Hatha yoga has a wide variety of styles and approaches that range from very strenuous to quite gentle and relaxing. All forms increase strength and flexibility.

The yoga workout on the DVD included with this book is specifically designed for figure skaters. In addition to helping you feel more relaxed, you will find that this workout will also increase your flexibility, extension, and isometric strength.

Mind-to-Muscle Techniques

Meditation

Meditation is perhaps the most pure form of *mind-to-muscle* relaxation. It is often used in yoga practice, but it may be performed on its own as well. Following are some of the basic steps to help you begin a meditation practice.

First, select a quiet environment. When you're first learning how to meditate, it is best to reduce the distraction potential as much as possible. Turn off your phone, put a "do not disturb" sign on the door, and take steps to make sure you are not interrupted. Eventually, you will want to transition to noisier environments. The world is not a silent place, and learning to mediate with some background noise is a valuable practice.

Choose a comfortable seated position with your back supported if necessary. Meditative posture is usually seated to prevent you from falling asleep. Select a position that you can maintain for at least 10 minutes to begin with. Sitting tall is most comfortable and conducive to an alert mental state. Close your eyes or keep them focused on a point in front of you. Sometimes, a visual focus or gazing point (in yoga referred to as a *drishti*), such as a candle, is useful to focus attention.

Now, choose a mental focus—a suggestive word or phrase such as *relax, breathe,* or *let go*. A short line or phrase from a favorite prayer works well too. Next, relax your body with a minute or two of physical relaxation and breathing awareness. With a quick body scan and a few deep breaths, you can lower your physiological arousal and bring your awareness into the present moment. The mental focus is often coordinated with the breath.

Attempt to maintain a passive attitude toward meditating. In other words, don't let your judgmental mind interfere with your mediation practice. The harder you try and the more harshly you criticize your wandering mind, the farther you stray from the relaxation response. The first minute or two might seem easy, then your mind begins to wander until your thoughts sound something like, "Relax, relax, I'm doing it. Is 10 minutes up yet? Nope, nine more minutes to go…relax…I hope I remembered to turn out the back porch light. Oops, I'm not doing it anymore." When your mind starts to wander, simply bring your attention back to your focus, without judgment, scolding, or frustration.

Like most everything, mediation gets easier with practice. Practice is essential to gain the relaxation benefits. If you are new to meditation, start with one 10-minute session per day a few days a week, gradually increasing the time to 15 to 20 minutes and adding more days when you are ready. How will you know when the time is up? Place a clock within your peripheral vision and sneak a glance at it periodically. (Setting an alarm ruins your relaxation.)

Visualization

Visualization was first introduced as imagery and refers to the ability to make something real in your mind's eye. When you combine your imagination with a meditation-like focus, you are using visualization techniques. You have probably already had experience visualizing something you want to come true or things you are afraid of.

Visualization improves your ability to concentrate on one thing at a time (uni-tasking), and thus, it enhances the quality of your work or performance in any area. It also turns down the volume of that constant "mind chatter" that can get in the way of problem solving, clear thinking, and performance.

Visualization is commonly used for stress management as well as for success in athletic competition. It also can help when making a commitment to positive behavior change such as committing to training regularly, choosing healthful foods, or getting better grades in school. When you set behavior change goals and see yourself achieving these goals, your motivation and chances of success improve. Visualization may also help you to have a more positive outlook and self-concept, changing how you talk to yourself and perceive events around you.

When you begin a visualization practice, lie down in a comfortable, quiet place. Let your eyes close. You might choose to begin with a physical relaxation technique such as a body scan or deep breathing to relax your body and mind. Focus on whichever visualization technique you have decided to practice, using all of your senses to make the images as real as possible in your mind's eye.

If you find that you enjoy visualization, be sure to practice regularly. It may take time and practice to create effective images for your visualization practice. Make your images as believable and real as possible, as if they are already a reality. If they are too phony, your subconscious mind will reject them. Once your visualization skills are finely honed, you will be able to use them to relax, to energize, and to prepare for practice and competition.

Autogenic Training

Autogenic training is a form of auto- or self-hypnosis intended to induce the relaxation response. It consists of a series of suggestions meant to produce the physical sensations of heaviness and warmth. It can be performed lying down or in a seated position with the head, back, arms, and, if possible, the legs supported.

When practicing, close your eyes to better visualize or imagine the physical sensations. As you repeat each phrase, try to visualize the sensation being described, and make it real in your body. For example, as you repeat "My right arm is heavy," you might imagine that your right arm is made of lead and is so heavy you're not able to lift it. Don't force, *imagine*, and try *not* to try. Just observe your visualization with the same passive, non-judging awareness that you use with other relaxation techniques.

The Application Exercises include an autogenic training protocol that you may eventually choose to say in your head to truly experience self-hypnosis. Begin your practice by relaxing, then start repeating the phrases silently to yourself. You may wish to add some general suggestions, such as "My whole body feels quiet, heavy, comfortable, and relaxed," or "My mind is calm and quiet," or "I feel calm and quiet."

When you have achieved deep relaxation, you may also wish to use positive suggestions (also called affirmations) to help with changes you wish to make. Affirmations should be believable and brief (e.g., "I practice hard and am getting stronger every day"), to encourage sticking to your training schedule. Finish a session by repeating this phrase, "When I open my eyes, I will feel refreshed and alert." Give your muscles a stretch and bring your awareness back to your regular activities.

Positive Affirmations

Positive affirmations are positive statements that reinforce what you are trying to accomplish. If your goal is to prepare yourself for competition and you need to get relaxed and focused, an affirmation that is repeated over and over again can become another form of self-hypnosis. When you say your affirmation to yourself, say it in the present tense, as though your goal is already achieved. By doing so, you are focusing on your goal's potential for present reality. If you think of it as something that will happen later, later may never come. For example, "I land my double Axels cleanly" has more influence than "I will land my double Axel in this program run-through."

Make sure that you phrase your affirmations positively. Say something like "I *land* my double jumps," rather than "I *won't fall* on my double jumps." These phrases should be short, simple, and direct. Too many words make affirmations less useful. Choose your wording carefully so that it resonates with you. If you think the affirmation sounds stupid or silly, it won't be believable and your mind will reject it.

As you practice your affirmations, keep in mind that you are creating something new, not redoing what currently exists. Adopt the attitude that you accept what currently exists while creating a better future. This attitude prevents you from getting stuck in a conflict with your present reality and focusing on the opposite of what you want.

You may be thinking to yourself, isn't using this technique like being in denial about something? Affirmations are not intended to repress negative feelings. Just as you observe your thoughts and feelings during mindfulness meditation, you also observe your feelings during affirmation practice. Even negative thoughts and feelings have an important message that must be acknowledged. When repeating your affirmations during relaxation, try to believe them, even if only for a few moments.

Whether you're utilizing muscle-to-mind or mind-to-muscle techniques, finding relaxation techniques that work for you can tremendously enhance your sport performance and experience. In addition, learning how to decrease your stress levels has tremendous health benefits. Take some to time to learn and practice these techniques, both on their own and while you are practicing on-ice.

Jason R. Ross

Whether you're utilizing muscle-to-mind or mind-to-muscle techniques, finding relaxation techniques that work for you can tremendously enhance your sport performance and experience.

Application Exercises

Exercise 1: Relaxation Practice

Use the following questions to help you make a plan for relaxation practice:
- How might regular relaxation practice be beneficial for you?
- What is the best time for daily relaxation practice?
- Where will you practice? How will you avoid interruptions (e.g., unplug the phone, find a time when few people are home)?
- What problems (real or perceived) might encourage you to skip your relaxation practice? Describe how you might deal with each problem.

Some skaters find that recording their relaxation practice helps them follow through with their plans to find a technique that works. In your journal, record the date and time of practice and any other observations or thoughts that come to you.

Exercise 2: Meditation and Visualization

Use the following questions to help you make a plan for practicing meditation and visualization, and record your practice in your journal:
- How could meditation and visualization practice be most beneficial for you?
- Which techniques seem most interesting or useful to you?
- What is the best time for daily practice?
- Where will you practice? How will you avoid interruptions?
- What problems (real or perceived) might encourage you to skip your meditation and visualization practice? Describe how you might deal with each problem.

Exercise 3: Sample Progressive Relaxation Protocol

The following exercise is one example of a progressive relaxation protocol. You might choose just to read it over and memorize it. Or you might have someone read it aloud or record it so that you can hear the instructions as you follow along. When you are tightening the muscles, tense them for five to seven seconds. When you are relaxing the muscles, let them relax for 20 to 30 seconds. Focus on the feelings and sensations of tightening and relaxing your muscles.

Starting with the arms and hands: Contract both arms and hands by making fists and tightening your biceps and triceps, like a bodybuilder flexing his arm muscles. Then, release. Next, tighten the muscles in your face and neck. Wrinkle your forehead, squeeze your eyes shut, press your lips together, clench your teeth, and press your tongue against the roof of your mouth. Now, contract your neck muscles. Hold and release. Now, take a deep breath and hold it as you arch your back. Release.

Take another deep breath and hold as you tighten your abdominal muscles and press your lower back into the floor or chair. Relax. Now, pull your feet and toes up toward the knees and tighten the muscles in the front of your legs, your shins, and your quads. Release. Now, point your toes down and tighten the muscles on the backs of your legs and buttocks. Release and relax.

Exercise 4: Sample Autogenic Training Protocol

The following sample protocol has six stages consisting of a series of exercises that are meant to produce the physical sensations of warmth and heaviness and cause you to feel calm and relaxed. Learn each stage before progressing to the next stage.

Stage 1: Passively focus your attention on your dominant arm while silently saying, "My right/left arm is very heavy." Repeat this phrase to yourself six times. Next, say, "I am very calm" or "I am at peace." Then, cancel out the feeling of heaviness by bending your arm, taking a deep breath, and opening your eyes. Practice just this much until you can feel the heaviness start to spread to the opposite arm. When this sensation happens, replace "My right arm" with "My arms." Once the heaviness starts to spread to the legs, replace with "My arms and legs are heavy." Eventually, the entire body starts to feel heavy. If the mind wanders, passively redirect it back to the protocol. Once the heaviness experience can be produced at will, you're ready to move to the second stage.

Stage 2: The instructions at this stage are the same as for Stage 1, except the feelings of heaviness are replaced with warmth. Your practice will now start with this phrase, "My arms and legs are warm," (repeated six times), followed by "I am very quiet" or "I am at peace." "My right arm is warm," (repeated six times), followed by "I am very quiet" or "I am at peace." Once the sensations of heaviness and warmth have been mastered, you're ready for the third stage.

Stage 3: This stage introduces regulation of your heartbeat. The autosuggestion you'll use may be, "My heartbeat is regular and strong" or "My heart is beating quietly and strongly." The autosuggestions for this stage would still begin with the phrase, "My arms and legs are heavy." The same procedure occurs for the remaining stages, with the additional autosuggestions added at each stage.

Stage 4: This stage introduces regulation of your breathing rate. The usual autosuggestion at this stage is, "My breathing is slow, calm, and relaxed."

Stage 5: This stage introduces the sensation of warmth in the solar plexus. Use the autosuggestion, "My solar plexus is warm." You might also place your hand on your solar plexus as you say this phrase to yourself.

Stage 6: The final stage introduces coolness of the forehead. At this point, your autosuggestions are:

- "My arms and legs are heavy." (repeated six times)
- "I am very quiet."
- "My arms and legs are very warm." (repeated six times)
- "I am very quiet."
- "My heartbeat is regular and calm." (repeated six times)
- "I am very quiet."
- "My breathing is slow, calm, and relaxed." (repeated six times)
- "I am very quiet."
- "My solar plexus is warm." (repeated six times)
- "I am very quiet."
- "My forehead is cool." (repeated six times)
- "I am very quiet."

Energy and Arousal Activation Techniques

In the last chapter, you learned how to calm yourself down and relax. Relaxation techniques are great to use if you're feeling nervous, stressed, or just simply agitated. But you've probably also experienced the opposite kinds of feelings, where you feel slow, sluggish, and low on energy. In those cases, you're still not at your ideal energy level—you are in need of some energy or arousal activation.

Building on the previous chapter, this chapter introduces techniques meant to activate you or get you "psyched up" for practice and competition. You will learn techniques for creating and sustaining energy when you feel tired or burned out. You will also learn how to reach and sustain your optimal energy level so that you can compete at your best.

You've learned that when you relax, your heart rate and respiration rate slow down. Figure skating is an intense, competitive sport. To skate effectively, you need to skate quickly. If you are too relaxed, you can't perform at your best. Being able to increase your heart rate and breathing rate to get your physiological systems ready for action is an essential skill for generating energy on short notice or when brief bursts of energy are needed.

You can also use energizing techniques to reduce fatigue. You might find yourself getting tired during a long practice session when you're putting forth a lot of effort. Perhaps you've found yourself fatiguing during programs in past competitions. Skating requires physical stamina at very high, anaerobic levels. Identifying primary energizing techniques that tend to work for you, and having a few back-up techniques as well, will ensure that you can bring yourself to the appropriate energy levels that you need to get the most out of practice and during competition.

Getting Started

First, you need to be able to identify when you need to be energized, in general as well as in specific situations within the sport. Take a moment to consider those instances where you will need to either get yourself energized or get your energy back when you begin to fatigue. Next, you need to become aware of the signs and symptoms of low energy and activation, in terms of what happens in your body. For example, you might need to learn how to energize heavy legs for the required jumps in your program, or settle tremors in the body during spiral sequences. In the latter instance, your energy focus will be placing all available energy into extending through the arms and legs, away from your center, holding still but dynamically tensed.

Once you're able to identify the appropriate energy level and where to send that energy, the next step is to choose strategies that you can use to get "psyched up." Like the relaxation strategies, these strategies can be divided into the muscle-to-mind and mind-to-muscle categories.

Muscle-to-Mind Techniques

Many of these techniques will be familiar to you, but they are used in this context for the purposes of building energy or activation. They include doing breathing exercises, completing a pre-competition workout, improving pacing, and controlling physiological responses.

Breathing Exercises

Breathing control and focus are just as effective in producing energy as they are in reducing tension. The following breathing exercises are very effective in increasing energy levels on demand:

Increasing Respiration Rate

Begin in a comfortable position, focusing on a regular, relaxed breathing rhythm. After about five breaths, consciously increase that rhythm and imagine that with each breath, you are inhaling energy, and with each exhale, you are ridding your body of any waste products, fatigue, or anything else that may slow you down. Feel yourself being in full control, allowing your breath to supply the appropriate amount of oxygen and energy to perform at your best. As your breathing rate increases, your energy level increases.

Warming Single-Nostril Breathing

Get comfortable in a seated or supine position, and become aware of your breathing. Begin to regulate your breathing by making the inhalations the same length as the exhalations. Place the first two fingers of the right hand between the eyebrows, while keeping the thumb, ring finger, and pinkie extended. From here, close the left nostril with the right ring finger. Inhale through the right nostril. At the top of the inhale, close the right nostril with the right thumb, open the left nostril, and then exhale through the left nostril. Repeat this pattern for 5 to 10 rounds. After the last exhale, take your hand away from your nose, and finish with regulated, even breathing.

Breath of Fire

Breath of fire is traditionally used in yoga classes as a means of stimulating the nervous system and cleansing the respiratory system. Find a comfortable and steady position. Begin inhaling through the nose, keeping the mouth closed. Exhale half of the air out of the lungs to a state somewhere between inhale and exhale. Exhale the remaining breath by quickly and sharply contracting the abdominal muscles. Exhalations should be short, vigorous, and active, while inhalations should be light and passive. Continue actively exhaling and passively inhaling, creating a rhythmic pattern for about 20 to 25 breaths. Repeat this technique two to five more times, and then finish with regulated, even breathing.

© Tom Theobald/ZUMA Press

Breathing control and focus are just as effective in producing energy as they are in reducing tension.

Pre-Competition Workout

Research has shown that working out or practicing before a competition may have a benefit in terms of helping with energy activation. This idea suggests that another effective muscle-to-mind technique is to do a workout before competition. Working out reduces feelings of tension and anxiety, which can easily hamper performance. Practicing or exercising in the hours prior to a competition may not enhance your actual skating performance from a physical perspective. However, it will not hurt your performance, and it does appear to enhance and increase activation, thereby reducing pre-competitive anxiety and nerves.

Improving Pacing

You may find yourself lacking energy in many cases because of fatigue. You may train hard without considering how to pace yourself, which can result in an unnecessary source of energy drain. Sometimes coaches will notice this drain and comment on it, but you will need to be able to self-monitor how hard you're pushing yourself during practice to make sure you're not practicing so hard that you can't practice effectively. You can learn how to ration your energy over time and improve on it with off-ice conditioning. You can also develop your self-awareness skills and become more sensitive to physical signs and symptoms of practicing at an appropriate energy level versus pushing to fatigue.

You can improve your pacing by identifying other unnecessary sources of energy drain and eliminating them as well. Some examples include too much muscle tension for a particular skill or situation, anger, frustration, and anxiety or worry over your performance. The mind-to-muscle section describes a technique for taking emotional responses that have the potential to drain you, and turning them around to work for you.

Controlling Physiological Responses

Another valuable skill to have for energy activation purposes is the ability to control your physiological responses. A skater must summon the energy to skate quickly in preparation for a triple jump, and then, very soon after, perform a complex footwork sequence, enter and exit a high-speed spin, and then, perhaps hold a static spiral position for several seconds, all while making it look smooth and easy.

Biofeedback has been demonstrated to be a very effective means of teaching athletes how to recognize and control physiological responses. For a skater, a heart rate monitor is a great tool, not only for cardiorespiratory conditioning, but also as a biofeedback mechanism to help you become aware of how you feel at different levels of energy exertion. It allows you to put a number or range of numbers (i.e., your heart rate) to those specific bodily sensations so you can repeat them and verify that you're recreating that same energy level. It can help you determine your optimal level (i.e., your heart rate when skating at your best) and help you monitor when you're working too hard or not hard enough. After a while, you will be able to regulate these responses using the various techniques for increasing or decreasing energy.

Mind-to-Muscle Techniques

The following techniques start with the mind and then manifest themselves by creating more energy for the body. Again, some of these techniques are familiar to you in other contexts, but they are used in this case for energy activation.

Imagery

Imagery can help you think more clearly, but it also can be used for motivation. It is the motivational function that makes imagery an effective means of energy enhancement. As you prepare for a triple lutz, you visualize yourself extending through the free leg, planting the toe pick, and exploding into the air. You see yourself in the air, pulled in tight in perfect flight position. As you land, you feel your landing leg touch down gracefully as your free leg extends out into a beautiful landing position. Visualizing successful outcomes in situations requiring activation and strong effort is motivating and energizing.

You can use other types of images to generate energy at will. For example, you might imagine yourself as a bull in a pen that is just about to be released to run the

Jason R. Ross

Imagery exercises are best practiced when you are stretching after a skating session or at other times when you can focus your attention internally.

streets of Spain, building up speed, strength, and power with each deep breath. Literally, thousands of images can be used as cues for generating energy: animals, machines, forces of nature, and so on. Think about what is meaningful to you to get your blood pumping and your heart going. Develop a ready supply of imagery cues that work for you in the various energy activation situations you encounter during practice, competition, and in the rest of your life. In your journal, create a plan for using these cues ahead of time, and be sure to include time to practice so that you're prepared to use them on a regular basis. Think about the times in your practice sessions when there might be brief lapses in action. These times may be the best times to use cues for activation and energizing. However, you should train your imagery energizing skills so that they are available to you whenever you need them. They are particularly effective to use when fatigue is beginning to set in, when something unexpected has happened (such as a fall, collision or wardrobe malfunction), or when a sudden burst of energy is needed to finish a program or performance. Remember to practice using your imagery skills during your skating practice sessions, and record in your journal your progress in using these skills appropriately during practice sessions.

In addition to on-ice imagery cues, imagery exercises can be performed off-ice. They are best practiced when you are stretching after a skating session or at other times when you can focus your attention internally. Think of this activity as creating an imaginary place in your mind where you can go to build optimal arousal/energy, repeat personal affirmations, focus on your goals for an upcoming competition, or use any other mental strategy that you find helpful. The key is to create an image that is controllable and meaningful to you and to use imagery practice to view the place as familiar and comfortable, where you can always go to in your mind to gain control of your physical and mental arousal levels.

Goal Setting and Other Self-Talk

Goal setting is another psychological skill that athletes use for motivation and energizing for an upcoming practice or competition. You've learned about goal setting for the season and for practice, but for the purposes of energy activation, these goals are much more immediate and are phrased silently or verbally just before the event occurs. Goal setting that occurs right before an event is positive self-talk that specifies the goal parameters. For example, just before you start your straight-line footwork, your stated goal might be, "Crisp edges." If you're been having difficulty centering your spins, you might state, "Tiny circles" as your goal right before entering your combination spin. Goal setting, even in immediate situations, is highly motivating and energizing and should be used often.

Remember from the chapter on positive practice that self-talk always should be stated positively. You might even choose to write down some of these goals and other self-talk cues in your journal and rehearse them even when you're not skating. Plan to practice them during skating practice as well, using them when you need to generate greater energy. As you reach that spot on the ice where you perform your double Axel, see the spot and think, *explode*. As you change edges during your spiral sequence, think, extend. Other key words that athletes use to symbolize greater energy and activation include *now, go, deep, hit*, and *power*. Choose energizing cues that are meaningful to you.

Transferring Energy

Throughout your day, your energy levels vary and change to meet the demands of what you're doing or thinking. Another helpful mind-to-muscle technique is learning how to convert energy from other sources into a positive and useful force for athletic performance. In addition to getting rid of the debilitating effect that negative emotions can have on performance, the act of converting aggression, anger, frustration, or some other emotion into energy to accomplish performance goals has a positive effect on performance. This technique is often referred to as "channeling" energy. As in the thought-stopping technique from the chapter on positive practice, the first step in converting negative energy into positive energy is to recognize that it's occurring. Stop the negative emotion using your stop signal, and then, immediately follow that signal with an energizing cue from the previous section. You may be surprised at how effective this technique can be. It is especially useful for people who tend to be more highly emotive in general and perhaps more emotionally connected to their skating.

Another way that energy can be converted is drawing it from sources outside of yourself. Figure skating is about performance, and your spectators truly appreciate you when you skate your best. You can draw energy from the audience by tuning them in, rather than tuning them out. Use their energy to inspire both you and your use of imagery, key words, cues, self-talk, and other psychological skills as you perform your programs. You also can draw energy from other skaters, particularly when it appears that they have momentum going for them.

Music also provides outside energy that you can channel inward, whether it's your skating music or other music that you've come to associate with getting pumped up. Many skaters have their own portable music devices that they use with headphones to set the appropriate arousal level they need to perform at their best. This option is a better choice than having loud music blaring over speakers in your warm-up area. The headphones may help you focus by providing the psychological association of staying "within your own head" as you prepare for competition.

One last way to transfer energy that's effective if you're feeling fatigued is to focus your attention away from the state of fatigue being experienced. Some skaters do just the opposite—as they become more tired, they focus on how tired they are. Doing so increases how tired you feel and results in poor performance. Instead, focus and concentrate on what is happening and what is about to happen in the current moment of your practice or competition. In cases of fatigue, it's more helpful to think about what you are doing rather than about how you are feeling.

To summarize, you've now learned how muscle-to-mind and mind-to-muscle techniques can be used for the purposes of creating energy when you are underactivated. As with the relaxation strategies, some of these strategies will likely resonate more with you than others. It's worthwhile to practice several techniques, rather than just focusing on one or two, so that the techniques are available for you in the moments where you need them the most.

Jason R. Ross

It's worthwhile to practice several relaxation techniques, rather than just focusing on one or two, so that the techniques are available for you in the moments where you need them the most.

Application Exercises

The following exercises will give you an opportunity to practice the skills and techniques taught in this chapter.

Exercise 1: Getting Started

Start a journal heading with the title *Energy Activation Strategies*. Create subheadings entitled *Times I Need to be Energized (General)* and *Times I Need to be Energized (Specific)*, and create lists of such times and instances under each heading. Write down the times or instances when you will need to either get yourself energized or get your energy back when you begin to fatigue. Now, create a third list, *Signs and Symptoms of Low Energy*, and write down what happens in your body when your energy is low.

Exercise 2: Commit to Practice

Give yourself some commitments in terms of how you will practice your energy activation skills. Write these commitments in your journal under your answers to Exercise 1. For example, you might start describing in your journal your energy level during a given practice and how you think it affected what you accomplished in practice. Or you may choose to practice a specific strategy, not only during skating, but also during other times in your life when you need more energy, so that you can get really good at making it happen when it needs to. Make at least two commitments to yourself that you will adhere to for the next three weeks.

Exercise 3: Practice Your Techniques

Choose at least three of the techniques described in this chapter to practice over the next three weeks. These techniques may or may not be tied into the commitments you made to yourself in the previous exercise. Record in your journal the technique you are practicing. Be sure to describe the technique, and record your progress on learning how to perform and use these techniques.

10

Techniques to Enhance Attention, Focus, and Concentration

Can you recall how many times in your life someone has asked you to pay attention? What about those times when your coach or someone else has asked you to focus or concentrate on what you're doing? Do you know exactly what those skills involve? Do you know when you're focusing and concentrating and when you're not? Can you make yourself pay attention, focus, or concentrate at will?

You've learned about attention, focus, and concentration in several other chapters in this book as they apply to practicing, becoming more relaxed, or becoming more energized. Because these skills are so important, this entire chapter is devoted to discussing the ability to pay attention, focus, concentrate, and reach that point where mind and body work together in what is known as *flow*.

Human beings have the ability to block out or ignore things around them while paying selective attention to information that is meaningful to what they're doing. Imagine what it would be like if you couldn't block things out. If you didn't have the ability to concentrate on one or two relevant things at a time, you simply could not function. Too many things in your internal and external worlds could potentially distract you. Fortunately, you do have this inherent ability—you may just need to hone it so that you can get it to work to your advantage while skating.

The ability to selectively attend to the specific things you think, sense, and feel while you're skating can help you improve the process of learning and refining your technique, as well as help you perform better during competition. If you can tune in to the feel of your edge on the ice and tune out the fall you just took, for example, your attention will be selectively attuned to the task at hand. Keeping yourself focused and in the moment can lead to some of the very best and most satisfying skating you are capable of. Some skaters are better than others at selectively attending to important internal and external cues, which is one way of distinguishing good athletes from elite ones. This ability may be partly biochemical in nature, meaning that in some cases the inability to selectively attend to instructions or cues is not always due to a lack of effort. Basically, every skater can learn how to focus, concentrate, and ultimately, perform at their optimal level.

Attentional Focus

Attentional focus is the term sport psychologists use to describe an athlete's ability to pay attention to appropriate cues during practice and competition. The concept of attentional focus refers to the ability to control attention in two ways, depending on the demands of the current situation: by making your attention narrow or broad at will, like a camera lens, and by directing your attention outward or inward. For example, any time you are skating by yourself on the ice, you can narrow your attention and draw it inside of yourself so that you are focusing only on yourself. However, you are most often practicing with other skaters, so you need to have a broader and more external focus to prevent colliding with other skaters. This example is a simple way of thinking about attentional focus. As you think more about this concept, you realize that attentional focus while skating is a little more complicated. To skate an effective program, your attentional focus must broaden and narrow and move from internal to external several times during your performance. For example, as you begin your program, you broaden your focus to draw energy from the audience and invite them into your world through your performance. As you skate your more challenging elements, you narrow your focus momentarily on the mechanics of the element, execute, and then, broaden again to acknowledge the audience.

Things inside and outside of yourself cue you in terms of how to focus your attention. These cues may be environmental, physical, or mental. Some cues are relevant and necessary for quality performance, while others are irrelevant and can damage performance. Your coach should not assume that you automatically know where to look or how to focus. If your coach doesn't already help in this area, encourage her to tell you what to focus on. Many coaches will create drills so that you can experience the optimal focus, if one exists for what you're doing. If an optimal focus does not exist, your coach can create drills that will help you find the focus that works best for you. Work with your coach to help you identify some of these cues for elements you're practicing, as well as for use during your programs.

Arousal Level and Attentional Focus

Arousal or energy level affects your ability to attend to relevant cues, which is another reason why it is so important to be able to determine your optimal level of arousal for practice and competition. Most research shows that when arousal or energy levels are too low, athletes tend to focus too broadly and pick up both relevant and irrelevant cues. Responding to irrelevant cues tends to result in a less successful performance. As athletes become more energized, their attention narrows. At some optimal point, attentional narrowing blocks out all of the unimportant things and allows only the important cues to remain. At this point, performance should be at its best. If arousal continues to increase, attention becomes too narrow, and some of the important cues get blocked out, which also results in a less successful performance.

High levels of arousal also may become distracting. In addition to blocking out potentially helpful cues, being too energized decreases your ability to selectively attend to one thing at a time. Instead, your attention tends to shift randomly, decreasing your ability to focus on what matters. If you become distracted, it's usually very noticeable in your performance.

Performing in an athletic activity requires the athlete to narrowly focus upon the task at hand to realize success. Quality attentional focus can block out distractions and irrelevant cues and can even bring you back if your arousal levels start to increase unexpectedly. As the time to execute a skill gets closer, the requirement to narrowly focus your attention increases.

Attentional Control Training

In attentional control (also known as concentration) training, knowing what to focus on is as critical as knowing how to control your focus. You may have excellent concentration skills, but if you are focusing on the wrong things, the skills will not be helpful. The expanding awareness exercise included in the Application Exercises at the end of this chapter allows you to experience changing your attentional focus. This exercise can be practiced in its entirety or section by section and should be practiced either seated or lying down in a comfortable position.

Once you've developed your awareness to the level that allows you to tune into important internal and external cues, you then need to be able to hold your attention or concentration for the duration of the task demand—otherwise referred to as *staying in the moment*. Following are several strategies that you may try to enhance your concentration skills, either on or off the ice.

On-Ice Strategies

Rehearsal

Rehearsing and practicing does not generally mean the same thing. When you practice, you warm up, practice elements on their own, perhaps work on your endurance, power, and any number of other things. When you rehearse, you are practicing specifically the way you intend to perform. Rehearsing is an important focusing strategy that you can use to control attention during practice. Dress rehearsals are discussed in detail in the last chapter, and they are a key aspect of preparing for success in competition. Rehearsals also should be used to ready yourself for other competition experiences such as responding to competitors and the media after a variety of different competitive outcomes. Be sure to rehearse how to react successfully to conditions under which you have fallen on jumps or made errors on other elements.

Positive Self-Talk

Positive self-talk can be used as an attentional strategy to help you focus on positive thoughts and behaviors. You've already learned how to use self-talk to stop negative thoughts and to focus on positive thoughts. To overcome feelings of self-doubt and anxiety, it is necessary to apply the principles of selective attention and to approach every skating situation with a positive attitude and belief that you will succeed. When negative thoughts come into your consciousness, remove or displace them with positive thoughts using the thought-stopping technique that was discussed in a previous chapter.

Attentional Cues and Triggers

Develop key word cues that utilize the three Ps: positive, present, and process. When developing cues for a program, think about each element and what your focus should be at that time. What cue word or words match that focus? Now, picture your program as the judges would see it, and see if the cues that you came up with still apply. To get a third perspective, review videotape with your coach to see if the cues still apply.

Imagery

Use imagery to focus your attention during practice. You can turn failure into success by imagining performing an element perfectly as soon as possible after making an error and before making another attempt. Before skating a program run-through, visualize the program skated the way you want to skate it, performing a perfect run-through in your head just before performing it on the ice.

Off-Ice Strategies

Mindfulness Training

Mindfulness is often referred to as *uni-tasking* or focusing on one thing for an extended period of time. When you are mindful, you are in the moment. To experience this feeling, sit quietly, close your eyes, and see how long you can focus on a single thought. If you want to see if you're getting better at "locking in," start a stopwatch when you begin your mindfulness practice, and stop it as soon as you realize that your mind has started to wander.

Practicing Hatha Yoga Mindfully

You have already learned about the relaxation benefits of hatha yoga. You know that yoga is good for your body in terms of increasing strength and flexibility, alleviating stress, and, when practiced with the appropriate breathing techniques, improving the functioning of your cardiorespiratory system. Yoga, when practiced mindfully, also can improve your ability to focus. A good yoga teacher provides several cues that you can internalize as you perform the poses. Staying in the moment with each pose makes a yoga practice much more rewarding and only enhances the previously mentioned benefits.

One Pointing

Look at an action photo of your favorite figure skater. Focus on one aspect of that picture, as narrow as the toe pick on the left skate, for example. See how long you can remain focused on that particular aspect. If your mind wanders, don't criticize yourself, simply draw your attention back to your "one point" as soon as you notice you've lost concentration.

Puzzles and Crosswords

If you don't do so already, start completing puzzle books or playing simple, sequence-based computer games. These types of activities help you to focus on a pattern and move quickly through a sequence, just like when you skate a program or test your moves in the field. These games don't need to be fancy, and as you work through various ones, time yourself to see if you're getting faster. A sample activity is included in the Application Exercises at the end of this chapter.

Developing Performance Plans

You can learn to repeat your ideal performance state by associating becoming more focused with certain performance rituals. Performance plans are set routines that you establish for warm-ups, practices, and competitions. You learned about a pre-practice performance routine in the chapter on productive practice. A pre-competition plan, described in the last chapter, involves setting a routine to follow before every competition, starting as early as the night before the competition. The idea is to help you develop a pattern that prepares you to be your best for the competition and usually includes sleeping, eating, practicing, exercising, and preparing mentally (the pre-competition plan will be discussed more in the last chapter).

When Athletes Are in the Zone

No discussion of attention and concentration would be complete, from a mind-body perspective, without clarifying the phrase "in the zone," which has been used to refer to an extraordinary performance by an athlete. Some scientists describe this phenomenon in terms of *automaticity*, meaning that the skills are so well rehearsed that no thought or effort is required to perform them. It's the idea that when you're in the zone, you're somehow disconnected from interference of conscious thought.

Psychologists make a distinction between controlled and automatic processing of information. When you are learning a new element, you must think very deliberately about what you're doing. In other words, you focus on controlled processing of information. This concept means that you are paying attention to the details of executing the skill to be learned—almost all of your attention is focused on executing this skill to the exclusion of other important cues. Controlled processing is relatively slow and effortful, consuming most of your available "brain power," if you will.

Once the element is mastered, then it is controlled by automatic processing. You don't have to *think* about it anymore—you just do it. The execution of the skill is still being monitored by the brain, but because it is well learned, it requires little conscious attention. One of the weaknesses of automatic processing is in knowing whether the skill has reached the level of automaticity. If it's truly not at that level of mastery yet, it becomes susceptible to error if unexpected interference occurs during the execution of the skill. Some aspects of an activity can mask whether or not true mastery of a skill exists. For example, think about how skating a program, in theory, is similar to reciting the alphabet—the elements need to be done in sequence. If you get interrupted while reciting the alphabet and then are asked to begin again, or if you are asked to begin from some letter other than A, you often have to start over to get back on track. The chain of responses is interrupted, so you have to start back at a familiar place. This restarting is not an option in figure skating where it is imperative to pick up where you were and get back into the flow of the program with your music. It means that every element needs to be automatic on its own. You don't want to hesitate or entertain a negative thought because if you do, you may upset the automatic processing of the elements in the rest of your program.

Others believe that skilled athletic performance reflects close coordination between mind and body, and that it is an insult to the intelligence of athletes to suggest that their performances are due to automatic physical ability. The term *physical genius* has been used to describe elite athletes, gifted musicians, and top-level surgeons who have the following three characteristics in common (Gladwell, 1999). First, these kinds of people seem to be born with certain raw physical and mental abilities. Second, they spend time, literally thousands of hours, practicing (mentally and physically) to become the best at what they do. It is no accident that elite athletes often play in the zone—they spend so much time practicing that they have the potential to be in the zone every time they perform. The third characteristic is that they utilize their imaginations. According to Gladwell, who coined the term physical genius, top athletes imagine every possible situation that could occur in competition so they are not surprised by anything. Being a physical genius is not just about being in the zone—it is perfecting your game mentally and physically, so that you are in the zone when you need to be.

To skate a program perfectly requires a delicate interaction between the mind and body. Describing a peak performance as simply being in the zone, as if the mind is separate from the body, underscores all of the preparation that is required to become an elite athlete at any level of competition.

To skate a program perfectly requires a delicate interaction between the mind and body.

Flow: The Psychology of Optimal Experience

Flow is a concept that was developed by the psychologist Mihaly Csikszentmihalyi and refers to "a state of optimal experience involving total absorption in a task and creating a state of consciousness where optimal levels of function often occur" (Jackson, 1992). You experience flow when you are engaged in an interesting activity for its own sake and for no other reason or goal. If you truly enjoy skating just for the sake of skating, you are experiencing at least some level of flow.

Csikszentmihalyi (1990) lists the following nine defining characteristics of the flow experience:

- Requirement of a challenge/skill balance
- Merging of action and awareness (sense of automaticity and spontaneity)
- Goals that are clearly defined
- Clear, unambiguous feedback
- Total concentration on the skill being performed
- Sense of being in control without trying to be in control (paradox of control)
- Loss of self-awareness (becoming one with the activity)
- Loss of time awareness
- Autotelic experience (end result of all of the other characteristics)

Peak performance or peak experience is not the same as the flow experience. Flow is a combination of emotional ecstasy and personal best performance. You may skate your personal best in a competition, yet not really consider the total experience as a peak moment. On the other hand, you may experience the nine characteristics of flow listed previously and not receive a personal best score. In studying the flow experience with figure skaters, sport psychologist Susan Jackson identified factors believed to allow flow to happen (i.e., facilitate flow), as well as other factors believed to prevent flow (Figure 10-1) (Jackson, 1992, 1995).

© Tom Theobald/ZUMA Press

Peak performance or peak experience is not the same as the flow experience. Flow is a combination of emotional ecstasy and personal best performance.

Effect on Flow State	Factor
Facilitate	Development of a positive mental attitude
	Positive pre-competitive affect
	Positive competitive affect (during contest)
	Maintaining appropriate attentional focus
	Physical readiness (perception of being prepared)
	Unity with teammate(s) and/or coach
Prevent	Experiencing physical problems and mistakes
	Inability to maintain appropriate attentional focus
	Negative mental attitude
	Lack of audience response

Figure 10-1. Factors that affect flow states

Listed as the first of Csikszentmihalyi's characteristics, the flow experience occurs when positive interaction between skill and challenge exists. This concept is illustrated in Figure 10-2.

	High Challenge	Low Challenge
High Skill	Flow	Boredom
Low Skill	Anxiety	Apathy

Figure 10-2. Skill, challenge, and the flow experience

The flow experience is most likely to occur when you are highly skilled at the task, yet feel personally challenged by the competition that you face. If you feel challenged by the competition, and you also feel that your skills are not ready, anxiety is likely to occur. Boredom occurs when a highly-skilled athlete is not appropriately challenged. The last combination is apathy, which occurs when skill level is low and the task isn't particularly challenging.

In her interviews with elite, international-level figure skaters, Jackson found that specific psychological states coincided with the characteristics of flow. These skaters described feeling in complete control, having total confidence, being completely absorbed in the activity, and sensing that they "could do no wrong" (Jackson, 1992). The most distinguishing aspects of the flow experience for these athletes were merging action and awareness, maintaining task-focused concentration, and feeling in control without trying to be in control. Her research also showed that athletes who experience flow, compared to those who do not, have a higher level of self-confidence just prior to an event, a higher perceived ability, and lower anxiety. Jackson has found that athletes who believe in their capabilities are more likely to experience flow even when the challenge of a specific sport competition is high. These findings suggest that you can learn the prerequisite skills that may enhance the likeliness of experiencing flow. Learning to be confident (Chapter 11), focusing your attention on the task at hand (this chapter), controlling your anxiety (Chapter 8), and setting appropriate and challenging goals (Chapters 4 and 5) may enable you to experience flow and peak performance more often.

Enhancing your attention, focus, and concentration is a key element in improving all of your figure skating skills. Learning to become more aware and how to focus on what you are doing is time well spent. These skills can transfer to any other area of your life that requires close attention and focus, such as taking an important exam.

© Tom Theobald/ZUMA Press

Enhancing your attention, focus, and concentration is a key element in improving all of your figure skating skills.

Application Exercises

Exercise 1: Expanding Awareness

A sport psychologist named Eugene Gauron (1984) developed the following imagery exercise to help athletes expand their awareness. You can practice this exercise in its entirety or break the segments into separate exercises.

Begin by focusing on your breath. As you exhale, try to relax all of the muscles in your shoulders, chest, and neck. With each breath, try to make the exhalation longer than the inhalation. Then, after you've inhaled, pause for a moment before exhaling. Let the breath move your abdomen, putting little if any thought into the movement.

Now, shift your attention so that you're listening very closely to the sounds around you. Hear each sound separately, identify what is making the sound, and apply a mental label. For example, you might hear someone sneeze, the sound of a coach's voice, music, or any number of things. Next, broaden your focus so you hear all the sounds at once, without identifying or labeling individual sounds. Listen to the blend of sounds as you would listen to music, allowing your thoughts of anything else to drop away.

Next, turn your attention to the bodily sensations you're currently experiencing such as the feeling of the chair you're sitting on, the clothes on your body, and so forth. As with the sounds, mentally label each sensation one at a time. Take your time with this exercise, and consider the quality of the sensation and what outside factors are contributing. Then, experience all of these physical sensations together without letting one or the other stand out as distinct. Broadly sense how your body feels.

Now, turn your attention only to how you're thinking and feeling. Let each thought or emotion wash over you gently, without forcing. Identify what kinds of thoughts or feelings you're having, but stay calm even if they are unpleasant. Experience each thought and feeling one at a time. Then, try to empty yourself of your thoughts and feelings. If you're not able to do this part, then just focus on one thought or feeling and keep your attention there.

Now, open your eyes and choose an object directly across from you. While looking in the direction of that object, try to see as much of the room and other objects in the room as your peripheral vision will allow. Try to observe the entire room all at once. Now, picture yourself looking through a camera lens. Center the camera lens on the object across from you. Start to slowly narrow your focus on that object until you only see the object through a very small lens. Then, expand your focus again so that eventually you can see everything in the room again. Think of this change in focus like "zooming in" and "zooming out."

This exercise helps you experience different attentional styles, but it also helps you learn to keep focus in one place and then change across the internal to external dimension and from the specific to the panoramic focus. Make a commitment to practice this exercise at least once in the coming week.

Exercise 2: Grid Concentration Exercise

Use the sample concentration grid (Figure 10-3), or create a similar one (10 x 10) in your journal. If you are creating your own, randomly fill in each cell with a double-digit number, starting with 00 and going through 99. You may choose to make copies of this grid before marking on it.

00	39	11	75	64	30	48	02	36	13
21	80	56	18	59	16	71	54	10	42
90	07	32	51	26	94	06	93	22	83
12	86	15	44	61	67	87	38	46	03
65	24	35	76	01	82	77	95	60	27
70	52	29	57	47	96	20	99	73	50
28	91	41	81	92	05	66	40	89	17
45	09	63	37	23	72	98	79	25	55
04	85	78	53	88	31	14	58	49	68
34	97	19	69	43	74	33	84	62	08

Figure 10-3. Sample grid for concentration exercise

On your grid, find the lowest number and put a slash through it, continuing in ascending order until you have marked off each number. For training and assessing your ability to concentrate, use a timer or stopwatch to see how many numbers you can mark off in one minute. You are experiencing good concentration when you can mark off at least 20 to 30 numbers in one minute. See how quickly you can master the grid. Once your speed plateaus, repeat this exercise with other randomized grids to further improve your concentration and focus.

Exercise 3: Practicing the Techniques

Select at least two strategies discussed in this chapter for improving focus and concentration to practice over the next three weeks. Record your goals and progress in your journal.

11

Techniques to Improve Confidence

What comes to mind when you think of a self-confident person? What things tip you off that a person is self-confident? People who are self-confident believe in themselves and their abilities. They tend to be optimistic and to expect things to work out in their favor. They also believe in their ability to perform when they need to, a concept that psychologists refer to as *self-efficacy*. All of these things create that air that successful people seem to have, and this belief system is essential for success in figure skating. If you don't believe in yourself, you are giving the advantage to the skating competitors who do.

Understanding Confidence Self-Check

To get a sense of how much you understand about confidence, take this brief true or false self-check. Try to make your choices without looking ahead at the answers provided.

- True or False: Confidence is something you either have or you don't.
- True or False: When you win all the time, you will always be confident.
- True or False: Negative feedback can build confidence.
- True or False: Making mistakes can build confidence.
- True or False: Being confident means being conceited and thinking you're better than everyone else.

Answers

- True or False: Confidence is something you either have or you don't.

False. Confidence is a constructive way of thinking that anyone can learn. Constructive thinking means holding on to the thoughts that benefit you and letting go of those that simply bring you down. You gain confidence just like you gain any other skill—by making the commitment to change how you think, and then practicing thinking in this way.

- True or False: When you win all the time, you will always be confident.

False. Although past success can inspire future success, it does not guarantee it. As you progress in your competitive levels, you may find you're not as successful as you have been in the past and confidence that you may have had may now wane. Or, maybe you're a current champion and now have the extra pressure of having to defend your title. Maybe you're not able to let go of one particularly bad experience. Having winning ways does not necessarily guarantee having confidence.

- True or False: Negative feedback can build confidence.

True. The real issue with feedback is how you respond to criticism. It's natural to feel good about yourself when people compliment you. You also can choose to view criticism, sarcasm, and negative comments as challenges, and you can use them to build confidence. Instead of getting upset about receiving negative feedback, if you choose to respond by reinterpreting the comments or using active strategies to neutralize them, you may actually gain confidence. When you have the right attitude and thinking skills, you can gain confidence even when you have been passed over for a spot in the ice show, or when you have been told that you won't go very far in this sport, or when you have been disrespected, providing you know how to selectively reinterpret these experiences and take something constructive away from them.

- True or False: Making mistakes can build confidence.

True. No matter how hard or how often you train, you *will* make mistakes. The key is not responding to your mistakes by losing your confidence. If you tend to selectively pay more attention to your mistakes and errors, you become more cautious, tentative, and fearful. Even if you experience failure after failure, you can still build your confidence by choosing to pay attention to any small improvements and positive experiences that occur. You can learn to gain confidence even while making mistakes, which is what the best skaters in the world do.

- True or False: Being confident means being conceited and thinking you're better than everyone else.

False. Every sport has athletes who appear cocky and outspoken. Every sport also has representative athletes who carry themselves with a calm and quiet air of confidence. Think of how Michelle Kwan, the most decorated female singles figure skater in the history of U.S. Figure Skating, conducts herself as an ambassador for the sport of figure skating. You can be confident without being conceited or appearing as though you think you're better than others.

The idea with completing this self-check is to show you that confidence really isn't about what happens or doesn't happen. It has more to do with how you think, what you focus on, and how you react to the things that happen in your life.

Gaining Confidence: Getting Started

To get started on gaining confidence, make a commitment to concentrate on changing how you think so that you are focused on thinking positively. Chapter 6 was about positive thinking, so you already understand that the way you think affects how you perform. The thoughts you have about your abilities, the challenges you face, and the situations you find yourself in affect the way you feel at any time. As you learned in the chapters about arousal activation and deactivation, as well as in the chapter on attention, these feelings can produce changes in muscle tension, blood flow, hormone production, and your ability to stay focused. Confident athletes deliberately think positive thoughts that produce confident feelings, thereby improving their ability to perform.

Next, you need to start or continue being honest with yourself. If you are not self-aware or are not evaluating your thoughts honestly, your confidence will not increase. Rather than block out self-doubt and hesitation, discover when and why you're having those feelings. Having this skill will not only help improve your confidence and skating ability, but it will also aid you in other challenging areas of your life.

After you've made the commitment to change how you think and become more aware of negative thinking patterns, you then need to consider how you interpret the things that happen to you in your life. Psychologists refer to this ability as *explanatory style*. Do you see having success as something that will continue to happen or as a one-time fluke? Do you see your less successful experiences the same way? Do your successes affect other areas of your life? Do your failures affect other areas of your life? If you make a mistake early in a program, are you doomed to a poor performance? Are you responsible for your successes? What about your failures? Are your successes and failures within your control? The way you answer these types of questions defines your explanatory style, which may be more optimistic or pessimistic, depending on your answers.

Being optimistic in your explanatory style is not the same as being delusional. You shouldn't ignore mistakes entirely or adopt a totally unrealistic view of your skills or the circumstances. Instead, your explanatory style should allow you to view mistakes and failures productively, using them as tools for improvement. It's okay to criticize yourself occasionally, as long as you keep it in perspective. On the other hand, it is possible to become overly optimistic, where you lack true self-awareness about your skill and control. This attitude can lead to poor decision-making, which is why it's important to honestly reflect on your performance, using a variety of feedback methods (e.g., coaches, videotapes, comments from judges, friends, and family) and consider those rationally.

Confidence in competitive performance is the result of consistent, constructive thinking in how you view yourself, your sport, and your experiences as a figure skater. When you can consistently control your thoughts in these areas, you'll find that you experience more energy, optimism, and enthusiasm, which is partly what enables great athletes to be the best they can be. Unfortunately, lots of things in society can potentially unravel your confidence. To resist these negative aspects of socialization, you need to understand that high levels of performance and personal growth will not occur with a negative focus. Fortunately, if you already have a negative focus, you can learn to change it. The next section in this chapter revisits strategies you've used before, only with the goal of increasing your confidence in mind.

Developing Self-Confidence Through Monitoring Program Run-Throughs

Rehearsing and practicing to make sure your skills and technique are solid is one of the most important components of building confidence. You want to go into competition with the mindset of completing a program just as you would a high-quality run-through in practice. To ensure your success, begin scoring your practice program run-throughs during the month or so prior to an important competition. A sample scoring activity is included in the Application Exercises at the end of this chapter. Monitor your improvements to build confidence in your skills.

Developing Self-Confidence Through Imagery

Self-confidence is achieved by believing you are competent and successful. Imagery is a powerful technique that you can use to enhance your confidence—you should always imagine yourself as being competent and successful. It is especially useful to recreate past successful performances and internalize the positive feelings that accompanied those successes.

Another useful imagery practice is based on the *Idealized Self-Image* (ISI) exercise (Lazarus, 1984), which helps to build confidence and self-esteem. To practice this exercise, imagine yourself performing your program, displaying the physical and psychological skills and qualities that you would most like to have. This image should be very specific, not general as in, "I see myself performing well." Then, you should carefully compare and contrast your idealized self-image with your actual self-image. This exercise should help you understand the specific behaviors and thoughts that you can actively engage in to move toward your ideal.

Using Videos to Enhance Imagery

Videos can be used to help you gain confidence and improve your skills. Using videos of performances or practices where you demonstrated successful execution of elements and steady improvement can be used as positive feedback. Watching a well-executed element on video while recalling the emotions and sensations that accompanied the scenes serves as a form of imagery rehearsal, which can affect the body in many positive ways.

Videos also can be useful in helping to improve specific athletic skills. Watching video footage of an accomplished athlete successfully landing a clean double Axel or entering and exiting a perfectly centered combination spin can be very effective in improving your own skills and confidence level. The video will be especially effective if it includes multiple repetitions of a scene, separated by blank footage of equal time. As the screen goes blank after the scene, close your eyes and vividly imagine the same scene, feeling the emotions and sensations that accompany that execution. Open your eyes to view the next repetition of the scene, then close your eyes to imagine it, repeating this process through all the repetitions of the scene. This exercise can help you move toward the same expert level demonstrated in the video footage.

Developing Self-Confidence Through Self-Talk

You can use self-talk to build your confidence as well. As a psychological method for improving self-confidence, self-talk must be positive in nature, and it must lead to positive feelings about your abilities. Three types of self-talk used to build confidence include task-specific statements, encouragement and effort, and mood words.

Task-Specific Statements

This type of self-talk refers to words or statements that reinforce technique. For example, in a spin, the word circle might be used in association with staying centered and avoiding traveling.

Encouragement and Effort

This type of self-talk refers to words or statements that provide self-encouragement to persevere or try harder. For example, the phrase, "You can do it" might be used in preparation for a difficult jump.

Mood Word

This type of self-talk refers to words that set the stage for an increase in mood or arousal. For example, the mood words *soft* or *quick* might be used in conjunction with an arm position, knee position, or footwork sequence.

Regaining Confidence After an Injury

One particular type of situation in which skaters can lose confidence is when they get injured. A common psychological response to injury changes how you think and feel about your abilities in general and skating in particular. You might think about things like how the injury will affect your performance goals or how long it will take to recover, or you might even experience a sense of loss. You might think about who you are as a person (i.e., your self-worth), how the injury impacts that opinion, and how you plan to cope with that perception. These thoughts will impact not only how you respond emotionally to the injury, but also your behavioral response to the injury. It is common for athletes to have feelings of lower self-esteem and self-worth following a serious, sport-related injury, which, in turn, affects self-confidence. Self-confidence about skating performance may initially decline following an injury, but it can recover by the end of the rehabilitation phase.

Other common emotional responses to injury include fear of the unknown, anger, depression, frustration, and boredom associated with being injured. Although some athletes experience emotional problems that are significant enough to require professional care, most athletes only have temporary experiences with these feelings. The more competitive you are, the more you may initially experience higher levels of negative feelings associated with the injury, but you also will recover more quickly compared to recreational athletes. This idea suggests that the higher levels of negative feelings associated with injury might actually help by providing a faster recovery period. Perhaps the frustration and negative feelings provide increased motivation for you to work harder during the rehabilitation process.

It may seem that nothing good could come from an athletic injury, but this thought may not be entirely true. Successful recovery from an athletic injury is associated with several benefits, both in terms of personal growth and in performance enhancement in your ability to use your psychological skills. Some athletes even experience improvements in their physical and technical skills following an injury. Recovering from an injury is just a more extreme case where your psychological skills for building confidence can be put to the test.

Application Exercises

Exercise 1: Scoring Program Run-Throughs in Practice

Create a program run-through scoring sheet and use it to evaluate the quality of your program rehearsals. First, list the elements of your short and long programs in the left-hand column. Then, use the points system in Figure 11-1 to score all the elements after each program run-through. Be tough on yourself. Give yourself a 0 if an element was not attempted, and score it as X if it was attempted and completely missed (i.e., you popped it or fell).

Elements	Maximum Points	Deductions
Single Axel or double jump	1	-1/2 if two-footed, or hand down, or cheated
Double Axel or triple jump	2	-1 if two-footed, or hand down, or cheated
Jump combo	2	For each jump, -1/2 if two-footed, or hand down, or cheated
Double Axel or triple combo	3	For each jump, -1/2 if two-footed, or hand down, or cheated
Any combo spin	2	-1/2 if fewer than required revs on first spin -1/2 if fewer than required revs on second spin -1/2 if slow or poor position
Layback or flying spin	1	-1/2 if fewer than required revs -1/2 if slow or poor position or loss of balance -1/2 if leg not high enough or over hip level long enough
Spiral sequence	1	
Footwork	1	
All connecting steps done as as planned	1	

Figure 11-1. Program run-through scoring criteria

Situation	
Negative Thoughts	**Positive Thoughts**
You are expected to do well.	
I hope I don't blow it. I have to skate a clean short program. Some great skaters are here.	I'll do my own thing. Focus on what I can control. Skate like I do at a good practice run-through. I'll take it one step at a time.
You worry about what others will say if you skate poorly.	
Everyone will be asking, "What happened to you?" I can't let them down. Everyone will think I'm a loser.	I'll give 100% of my attention to skating. Tune out distractions, stay loose, and be positive. Focus on my skating. Let it go.
At the first practice at the competition, you see skaters landing difficult jumps.	
I can't believe how good they are. They're so much better than I am. I don't have a chance.	Let it go. I can't control what they do. I'll skate like a good practice run-through. I'll focus on what I can control.
Other skaters attempt to psych you out.	
They're so good. I don't have a chance. I hate braggarts. I'll have to skate better than I've ever skated.	Talk is cheap. I'll focus on my strengths. I'll focus on my own skating. I'll follow my competition plan.
Other skaters have more difficult content in their programs.	
Their programs are so much more difficult than mine. I'm going to have to be perfect. Even if I skate totally clean, I won't have a chance.	If I give 10% of my attention, they have 110% and I have 90%. My goal is to skate like a good practice run-through. Feel the edges and the music. Enjoy the experience of performing.
Your combination in your short program has been inconsistent in practices.	
I hope I don't blow my combo. If I miss the combo, I'm history. Everyone else is so consistent on their combo.	I'll focus on run-throughs where my combo was clean. I'll use my key words, set it up, and go for it. I've landed my combo in practices. I can do it here.
Skating order for the short program has been posted, and you have to skate first.	

Figure 11-2. Self-talk exercise

Situation	
Negative Thoughts	Positive Thoughts
The order for the long program has been posted, and you're the sixth skater in your flight.	
It's extremely important that you finish in the top three (to qualify for the next competition, to make a team, and so on).	
You have a bad warm-up right before you compete.	
The skater before you received very high scores.	
You fall on an early element in your program.	

Figure 11-2. Self-talk exercise (cont.)

Exercise 2: Strategies for Increasing Confidence

In your journal, describe the new strategies you will use for improving your confidence. How will you know that you are being honest with yourself and not delusional? How will you know if you're still being too hard on yourself?

Exercise 3: Using Self-Talk to Enhance Confidence in Key Situations

Examine each of the situations outlined in Figure 11-2 that you might experience before or during a competition. Put a star beside those situations that are specific to you, and feel free to write in others that may not be listed.

Rethink how you would use self-talk in each situation. The first few items in the first column may be similar to negative thoughts that you have in that situation. If they are similar, circle those negative thoughts, and then circle the positive thought you'll use instead. If the items are too different from your actual thoughts, feel free to write in your own negative and positive replacement thoughts. After the first few, start generating your own negative thoughts and replacement thoughts for the later situations and others that you think of on your own.

12

Effective Competition Preparation

In this final chapter, you'll learn how to effectively prepare for competition by performing off-ice program walk-throughs, on-ice run-throughs, and dress rehearsals using many of the psychological skills you have learned about in this book.

Practice Off-Ice Walk-Throughs During the Month Before a Competition

You can practice your competitive psychological skills by performing off-ice walk-throughs of your program. During a walk-through, while listening to the music for your program, try to feel yourself landing all the jumps, performing all the spins, and doing all the connecting steps in between. Research shows that skaters who practice walk-throughs have significantly more improvements in their jumps, spins, and connecting moves as compared to skaters who do not practice walk-throughs, even when the actual amount of on-ice practice for all skaters is the same. These results, and the results of similar studies of mental practice with athletes in other sports, clearly indicate that you can improve your performance at competition if, during the four weeks leading up to a competition, you do mental practice off-ice as well as doing program run-throughs on the ice.

For mental practice to be helpful, your off-ice walk-through must be done with considerable concentration. Before doing off-ice walk-throughs of your programs, diagram your programs on a sheet of paper that represents the ice surface, indicating where each of the elements should occur. Then, list your elements and one or two key words to help you get the proper feeling for each element. You may also write out some positive self-talk for some of the connecting moves in between elements to help you stay focused, stay in the moment, and feel the music and choreography.

Each time you do an off-ice walk-through, make it seem as real as possible. First, visualize yourself at the rink for an upcoming competition. Imagine that the skater before you has just finished. Feel yourself taking off your skate guards, stepping onto the ice, doing some stroking, performing a waltz jump or an Axel, or doing whatever you do to warm up. Visualize your coach at the skating door, and imagine yourself receiving last-minute encouragement from your coach. Imagine the marks being announced for the skaters before you, and imagine your name being announced. If someone is helping you do your walk-through, have that person announce the marks of another skater and then announce you as the next skater. Visualize the judging panel as you skate to your start position. From your start position, start your music, and walk out your program while saying your cue words and your self-talk out loud. Try to feel yourself setting up and landing all the jumps. Try to feel all the spins being done with high quality, and feel all the connecting steps and choreography in between.

For mental practice to help you improve, you must make it seem as real as possible, and you must imagine yourself skating well. Use the following checklist to monitor your progress. Answer each of the following questions with "yes," "somewhat," or "no." Did you:
- Visualize the rink, the audience, and the judges?
- Imagine that the skater before you just finished?
- Imagine yourself taking off your skate guards?
- Feel yourself stepping onto the ice?
- Feel the excitement that you normally feel?
- Feel yourself doing your usual mini on-ice warm-up?
- Imagine seeing and talking to your coach?
- Hear the marks of the preceding skater?
- Hear your name being announced?
- Feel yourself skating past the judges to your start position?
- Rehearse positive self-talk and take your start position?
- Listen to the music and walk out the program?
- Say your key words out loud?
- Say your self-talk out loud for connecting moves?
- Feel the edges and set up for jumps?
- Feel yourself landing your jumps?
- Feel yourself doing the spins well?

- Feel the choreography, soft knees, and positive and connecting steps?
- Feel the music and feel yourself presenting well?

Prepare and Follow a Pre-Skate Plan at Competitions

One study questioned former national U.S. champion figure skaters about their thoughts and feelings at important competitions. At competitions where they performed well, most of them reported:
- Having and following strategies to control anxiety and nervousness
- Using positive self-talk to focus on their strengths (rather than dwelling on a problem jump or a weakness)
- Focusing on skating well and not worrying about placing
- Having strategies to tune out skating when away from the rink during the days of the competition (rather than always thinking about skating)
- Being able to tune out distractions happening around them
- Focusing on a few key points during their programs and taking them one step at a time

At competitions where they performed poorly, most of them reported:
- Feeling affected by distractions (usually other people coming up and talking) and surprises just before performing
- Being unable to control nervousness
- Worrying about the outcome
- Experiencing negative self-talk about themselves
- Thinking about any mistakes that were made rather than moving on

From these kinds of studies with figure skaters as well as athletes in other sports, top athletes have learned to develop detailed competition plans to maximize their performances. Competition plans typically include the following:
- Time management plans for every day of the competition to stay positive, eat healthy, get lots of rest, be well organized, and tune out skating when away from the rink
- Pre-planned routines and positive thoughts for practice (at the competitions) to stay positive and remain focused
- A specific plan to control distractions and get back on track quickly if something doesn't go quite right
- A detailed mental preparation plan during the last hour or so before competing for stretching, warming up, waiting for your turn, and performing to maintain confidence and concentration and to control nervousness

A pre-skate plan will help you to:

- Ensure that you are appropriately warmed up and energized
- Minimize distracters that affect your concentration
- Have activities and self-talk available to maintain high confidence
- Eliminate negative thinking and anything else that makes you nervous
- Ensure that when you step on the ice to skate your program, you are ready to perform like you do during one of your better program run-throughs at practice

What Time Frame Does a Pre-Skate Plan Cover?

At a competition, your pre-skate plan can include the last hour or so before your on-ice warm-up and the time after you warm up while you are waiting for your turn to skate your program.

© Nancy Pastor/Washington Times/ZUMA Press

When you step on the ice to skate your program, be sure that you are ready to perform like you do during one of your better program run-throughs at practice.

What Goes Into a Pre-Skate Plan?

Pre-skate plans can include doing relaxation exercises, stretching, repeating positive self-talk, tuning out thoughts of skating with a portable music device and relaxing music, talking to your coach or others about non-skating activities, talking to people who help you think positively about your skating, doing an off-ice walk-through of your program, thinking relaxing thoughts to conserve energy, and doing other activities that can be repeatedly practiced at competitions. When preparing your pre-skate plan, it is important to remember that you don't want to think about your program during the last hour or so before you skate. It's impossible to concentrate effectively during that time, and attempting to do so will gradually increase nervousness. Instead, an important part of your pre-skate plan is to have activities to occupy your mind with things other than skating. One way of keeping your mind preoccupied is to stay in the present moment. For example, when stretching, focus on how your muscles feel. When listening to your favorite music, really get into the music. When putting on your costume, admire the texture and color and so on. Be really present and mindful.

When you prepare your pre-skate plan, make sure that you discuss it with your coach. For your plan to help you concentrate, maintain high confidence, stay relaxed, and think positively about an upcoming performance, it's very important that your coach is aware and supportive of your pre-skate plan.

Jason R. Ross

Pre-skate plans can include doing several things, including relaxation exercises, stretching, repeating positive self-talk, tuning out thoughts of skating with a portable music device and relaxing music.

General Organization at a Competition

The better prepared and organized you are, the better you will be able to control things that affect your performance. If you have not planned things out well, you stand a greater chance of outside distracters taking away from a top-level performance. Don't worry about things that are beyond your control such as the order in which you have to skate. Do prepare for things you can control. Shortly after registration, sit down with your coach and complete the following checklist:

• Check the practice and competition schedule.
• Check the bus or car schedules.
• Decide on times for leaving and arriving at the rink and the hotel.
• Decide on the best times for eating and sleeping.
• Write out your time management plan for the duration of the competition.

Just before or after your first practice in the competitive rink, take some time to explore the arena. Locate the best place to stretch before you warm up for your programs, and look for a place to wait (following your mental preparation plan and after the warm-up) until it's your turn to skate.

Prepare a pre-skate plan for the time prior to the warm-up. Given the program type and number of skaters in the flight, you can anticipate program length and judges time, and then determine approximately how much time will be needed for each skater. Determine what you will be doing while the other skaters are skating.

Prepare a pre-skate plan for after the warm-up as well. If you're the first skater after the warm-up, the plan is not a big issue. But if you're the last skater in your flight, a pre-skate plan becomes extremely important. In general, the longer you have to wait before you skate after the warm-up, the more important it is to have planned activities to stay reasonably loose and maintain your confidence. Consider the following questions:

© Tom Theobald/ZUMA Press

Just before or after your first practice in the competitive rink, take some time to explore the arena.

- If you are fifth in your flight, should you stand, walk, or sit?

Standing on skates is very different than actually skating. The muscles that help keep you balanced while standing get tired quickly and will tense up. If you have a short wait before your turn (perhaps up to eight or nine minutes), it's best to keep moving (e.g., walking or bouncing). But if you have a longer wait, sitting down is definitely the better option.

- Should you focus on your program while waiting?

If you have to wait more than 10 minutes before you skate, it's best not to think about skating and to think about things that will help you stay loose and relaxed. Some skaters use portable music devices, which is a great way to tune out thoughts of skating.

- How long do the benefits of a good warm-up last?

In terms of muscle physiology, a good warm-up definitely helps an athlete to perform better. However, if you do have a good warm-up and then wait longer than 10 minutes, the benefits of the warm-up are largely lost. Therefore, if you are skating last in your flight, you might want to begin moving and bouncing to simulate a mini off-ice warm-up during the second skater's program, using your portable music device to tune out the other skater's music.

If time allows, some skaters like to walk out their entire program one more time. That's certainly a possibility if you're the fourth, fifth, or sixth skater in your flight. However, some skaters perform better by tuning out skating altogether during the entire waiting period. They prefer to think about anything other than skating, to listen to music, to talk or joke with their coach or someone else about nonskating topics, etc. Use whichever approach works best for you.

As the skater before you begins her program, it's appropriate to return to the ice level. Spend those few minutes looking around at the audience, getting used to the atmosphere, and thinking about enjoying yourself on the ice and putting on a good show. If you think about skating at all during this time, it should be to focus only on the first element of your program. It is *not* recommended that you watch the skater who is skating before you. The two general rules for planning what you should do during your pre-skate period are as follows:
- Always do things that you have control over.
- Always do things that influence you in a positive way and help you stay loose and confident.

Application Exercise

Exercise 1: Create a Pre-Competition Plan

Using the information presented in this chapter, create a pre-competition plan to try out at your next competition. Be sure to include general organizational items as well as the specifics of your pre-skate plans, including what you will do both before and after your on-ice warm-up.

References

Csikszentmihalyi, M. (1990). *Flow: The Psychology of Optimal Experience*. New York, N.Y.: Harper and Row.

Gauron, E.F. (1984). *Mental Training for Peak Performance*. Lansing, NY: Sport Science Associates.

Gladwell, M. (1999). The physical genius. *The New Yorke*r, 75, 57-65.

Jackson, S.A. (1992). Athletes in flow: A qualitative investigation of flow states in elite figure skaters. *Journal of Applied Sport Psychology*, 4, 161-180.

Jackson, S.A. (1995). Factors influencing the occurrence of flow state in elite athletes. *Journal of Applied Sport Psychology*, 7, 138-166.

Lazarus, A. (1984). *In the Mind's Eye: The Power of Imagery for Personal Enrichment*. New York, N.Y.: Guildford.

Martin, G.L. (1998). *A Seasonal Sport Psychology Program for Figure Skaters: Mental Steps to Excellence*. Winnipeg, MB: Sport Science Press.

Poe, C.M. (2002). *Conditioning for Figure Skating: Off-Ice Techniques for On-Ice Performance*. Chicago, Ill.: Contemporary Books.

Ravizza, K. (2001). Increasing awareness for sport performance. In J. M. William's (Ed.) *Applied Sport Psychology: Personal Growth to Peak Performance* (4th ed.). Mountain View, Calif.: Mayfield Publishing Company.

Taylor, G.M. & Ste-Marie, D. M. (2001). Eating disorders symptoms in Canadian female pair and dance figure skaters. *International Journal of Sport Psychology*, 32, 21-28.

Vealey, R.S. & Greenleaf, C.A. (2001). Seeing is believing: Understanding and using imagery in sport. In J. M. William's (Ed.) *Applied Sport Psychology: Personal Growth to Peak Performance* (4th ed.). Mountain View, Calif.: Mayfield Publishing Company.

About the Author

Linda Ross, Ph.D., holds advanced degrees in both psychology and kinesiology. She is a lifelong athlete who has competed at the provincial/state, national, and international levels in several individual and team sports. She currently trains as an adult figure skater registered with U.S. Figure Skating. With over 25 years of experience in the health, wellness, and sport sciences industry, Linda is certified by the National Strength and Conditioning Association (NSCA), the American Council on Exercise (ACE), and the Aerobics and Fitness Association of America (AFAA). She lives in the greater Seattle, Washington, area with her husband and two dogs.